BENEDICT XVI

PRIESTS OF JESUS CHRIST

Pope Benedict XVI

PRIESTS OF JESUS CHRIST

REFLECTIONS ON THE PRIESTHOOD

*Extracts from his writings and speeches
selected by Fr Gerard Skinner*

FAMILY PUBLICATIONS

Papal Texts © Libreria Editrice Vaticana 2005-08
Design © Family Publications 2009
Cover Image © Stefano Spaziani 2008

ISBN 9781871217902

published by
Family Publications
Denis Riches House, 66 Sandford Lane
Kennington, Oxford OX1 5RP

Printed in Malta
through s|s|media ltd

Contents

Introduction

The reflections in this book are drawn from the writings of Pope Benedict XVI from the time of his election as Supreme Pontiff in April 2005 until the end of 2008. These writings have been arranged according to the style of delivery rather than thematically. A homily, for example, may touch on many interwoven themes pertinent to priesthood, the whole benefiting from not being broken up into its constituent parts.

In 1988 Cardinal Joseph Ratzinger published a collection of his meditations on the priesthood under the title *Ministers of Your Joy* of which he wrote, 'The theme that runs through all these reflections is the joy that comes from the Gospel.' Twenty years later this deep joy is evident throughout this volume too and is characterized by the repeated call of Pope Benedict for priests to become ever closer friends of the Lord. I hope that my selection from the Holy Father's most recent reflections on the priestly life does justice to his vision. I am certain that his words will inspire priests, seminarians, those discerning God's calling and many others, above all to give thanks to God for the gift of priests in the mystery of Jesus Christ.

Fr Gerard Skinner
London, Solemnity of All Saints, 2008

HOMILIES

I.
HOMILIES

Homily given at the

CHRISM MASS

*St Peter's Basilica
Holy Thursday, 13 April 2006*

In the hands of the Lord

Holy Thursday is the day on which the Lord gave the Twelve the priestly task of celebrating, in the bread and the wine, the Sacrament of his Body and Blood until he comes again. The paschal lamb and all the sacrifices of the Old Covenant are replaced by the gift of his Body and his Blood, the gift of himself.

Thus, the new worship was based on the fact that, in the first place, God makes a gift to us, and, filled with this gift, we become his: creation returns to the Creator.

So it is that the priesthood also became something new: it was no longer a question of lineage but of discovering oneself in the mystery of Jesus Christ. He is always the One who gives, who draws us to himself.

He alone can say: 'This is my Body . . . this is my Blood'. The mystery of the priesthood of the Church lies in the fact that we, miserable human beings, by virtue of the Sacrament, can speak with his '*I*': *in persona Christi.* He wishes to exercise *his* priesthood through us. On Holy Thursday, we remember in a special way this moving mystery, which moves us anew in every celebration of the Sacrament.

So that daily life will not dull what is great and mysterious, we need this specific commemoration, we need to return to that hour in which he placed his hands upon us and made us share in this mystery.

Let us reflect once again on the signs in which the Sacrament has been given to us. At the centre is the very ancient rite of the imposition of hands, with which he took possession of me, saying to me: 'You belong to me.'

However, in saying this he also said: 'You are under the protection of my hands. You are under the protection of my heart. You are kept safely in the palm of my hands, and this is precisely how you find yourself in the immensity of my love. Stay in my hands, and give me yours.'

Then let us remember that our hands were anointed with oil, which is the sign of the Holy Spirit and his power. Why one's hands? The human hand is the instrument of human action, it is the symbol of the human capacity to face the world, precisely to 'take it in hand'.

The Lord has laid his hands upon us and he now wants our hands so that they may become his own in the world. He no longer wants them to be instruments for taking things, people or the world for ourselves, to reduce them to being our possession, but instead, by putting ourselves at the service of his love, they can pass on his divine touch.

He wants our hands to be instruments of service, hence, an expression of the mission of the whole person who vouches for him and brings him to men and women. If human hands symbolically represent human faculties and, in general, the power skilfully to order the world, then anointed hands must be a sign of the human capacity for giving, for creativity in shaping the world with love. It is for this reason, of course, that we are in need of the Holy Spirit.

In the Old Testament, anointing is the sign of being taken into service: the king, the prophet, the priest, each does and gives more than what derives from himself alone. In a certain way, he is emptied of himself, so as to serve by making himself available to One who is greater than he.

If, in today's Gospel, Jesus presents himself as God's Anointed One, the Christ, then this itself means that he is acting for the Father's mission and in unity with the Holy Spirit. He is thereby giving the world a new kingship, a new priesthood, a new way of being a prophet who does not seek himself but lives for the One with a view to whom the world was created.

Today, let us once again put our hands at his disposal and pray to him to take us by the hand, again and again, and lead us.

In the sacramental gesture of the imposition of hands by the bishop, it was the Lord himself who laid his hands upon us. This sacramental sign sums up an entire existential process.

Once, like the first disciples, we encountered the Lord and heard his words: 'Follow me!' Perhaps, to start with, we followed him somewhat hesitantly, looking back and wondering if this really was the road for us. And at some point on the journey, we may have had the same experience as Peter after the miraculous catch; in other words, we may have been frightened by its size, by the size of the task and by the inadequacy of our own poor selves, so that we wanted to turn back. 'Depart from me, for I am a sinful man, O Lord' (Lk 5: 8).

Then, however, with great kindness, he took us by the hand, he drew us to himself and said to us: 'Do not fear! I am with you. I will not abandon you, do not leave me!'

And more than just once, the same thing that happened to Peter may have happened to us: while he was walking on the water towards the Lord, he suddenly realized that the water was not holding him up and that he was beginning to sink. And like Peter we cried, 'Lord, save me!' (Mt 14: 30). Seeing the elements raging on all sides, how could we get through the roaring, foaming waters of the past century, of the past millennium?

But then we looked towards him . . . and he grasped us by the hand and gave us a new 'specific weight': the lightness that derives from faith and draws us upwards. Then he stretched out to us the hand that sustains and carries us. He supports us. Let us fix our gaze ever anew on him and reach out to him. Let us allow his hand to take ours, and then we will not sink but will serve the life that is stronger than death and the love that is stronger than hatred.

Faith in Jesus, Son of the living God, is the means through which, time and again, we can take hold of Jesus' hand and in which he takes our hands and guides us.

One of my favourite prayers is the request that the liturgy puts on our lips before Communion: 'never let me be separated from you'. Let us ask that we never fall away from communion with his Body, with Christ himself, that we do not fall away from the Eucharistic mystery. Let us ask that he will never let go of our hands.

The Lord laid his hand upon us. He expressed the meaning of this gesture in these words: 'No longer do I call you servants, for the servant does not know what his master is doing; but I have called you friends, for all that I have heard from my Father I have made known to you' (Jn 15: 15). I no longer call you servants but friends: in these words one could actually perceive the institution of the priesthood. The Lord makes us his friends; he entrusts everything to us; he entrusts himself to us, so that we can speak with he himself – *in persona Christi capitis*.[1]

What trust! He has truly delivered himself into our hands. The essential signs of priestly ordination are basically all a manifestation of those words: the laying on of hands; the consignment of the book – of his words that he entrusts to us; the consignment of the chalice, with which he transmits to us his most profound and personal mystery.

---

1. "In the person of Christ the Head."

The power to absolve is part of all this. It also makes us share in his awareness of the misery of sin and of all the darkness in the world, and places in our hands the key to reopen the door to the Father's house.

I no longer call you servants but friends. This is the profound meaning of being a priest: becoming the friend of Jesus Christ. For this friendship we must daily recommit ourselves.

Friendship means sharing in thought and will. We must put into practice this communion of thought with Jesus, as St Paul tells us in his Letter to the Philippians (cf. 2: 2-5). And this communion of thought is not a purely intellectual thing, but a sharing of sentiments and will, hence, also of actions. This means that we should know Jesus in an increasingly personal way, listening to him, living together with him, staying with him.

Listening to him – in *lectio divina,* that is, reading Sacred Scripture in a non-academic but spiritual way; thus, we learn to encounter Jesus present, who speaks to us. We must reason and reflect, before him and with him, on his words and actions. The reading of Sacred Scripture is prayer, it must be prayer – it must emerge from prayer and lead to prayer.

The Evangelists tell us that the Lord frequently withdrew – for entire nights – 'to the mountains', to pray alone. We too need these 'mountains': they are inner peaks that we must scale, the mountain of prayer.

Only in this way does the friendship develop. Only in this way can we carry out our priestly service, only in this way can we take Christ and his Gospel to men and women.

Activism by itself can even be heroic, but in the end external action is fruitless and loses its effectiveness unless it is born from deep inner communion with Christ. The time we spend on this is truly a time of pastoral activity, authentic pastoral activity. The priest must above all be a man of prayer.

The world in its frenetic activism often loses its direction. Its action and capacities become destructive if they lack the power of prayer, from which flow the waters of life that irrigate the arid land.

I no longer call you servants, but friends. The core of the priesthood is being friends of Jesus Christ. Only in this way can we truly speak *in persona Christi*, even if our inner remoteness from Christ cannot jeopardize the validity of the Sacrament. Being a friend of Jesus, being a priest, means being a man of prayer. In this way we recognize him and emerge from the ignorance of simple servants. We thus learn to live, suffer and act with him and for him.

Being friends with Jesus is par excellence always friendship with his followers. We can be friends of Jesus only in communion with the whole of Christ, with the Head and with the Body; in the vigorous vine of the Church to which the Lord gives life.

Sacred Scripture is a living and actual Word, thanks to the Lord, only in her. Without the living subject of the Church that embraces the ages, more often than not the Bible would have splintered into heterogeneous writings and would thus have become a book of the past. It is eloquent in the present only where the 'Presence' is – where Christ remains for ever contemporary with us: in the Body of his Church.

Being a priest means becoming an ever closer friend of Jesus Christ with the whole of our existence. The world needs God – not just any god but the God of Jesus Christ, the God who made himself flesh and blood, who loved us to the point of dying for us, who rose and created within himself room for man. This God must live in us and we in him. This is our priestly call: only in this way can our action as priests bear fruit.

I would like to end this Homily with a word on Andrea Santoro, the priest from the Diocese of Rome who was assassinated in

Trebizond while he was praying.[2]

Cardinal Cé recounted to us during the Spiritual Exercises what Fr Santoro said. It reads: 'I am here to dwell among these people and enable Jesus to do so by lending him my flesh. . . . One becomes capable of salvation only by offering one's own flesh. The evil in the world must be borne and the pain shared, assimilating it into one's own flesh as did Jesus.'

Jesus assumed our flesh; let us give him our own. In this way he can come into the world and transform it. Amen!

---

2. Fr Andrea Santoro was a priest of the Diocese of Rome who had offered to work amongst the Catholic community in Trabzon, Turkey. On 6 February 2006 he was shot dead at the church of Santa Maria, Trabzon, whilst kneeling in prayer, by a sixteen year-old man.

Homily given at the

ORDINATION OF NEW PRIESTS FOR THE DIOCESE OF ROME

Vatican Basilica
Fourth Sunday of Easter, 7 May 2006

Shepherds with the Heart of Jesus

At this hour, dear friends, when you are being introduced as shepherds in the service of the Great Shepherd, Jesus Christ, through the Sacrament of Orders, it is the Lord himself who, in the Gospel, speaks of serving God's flock.[3]

The image of the shepherd comes from remote times. In the Orient of antiquity, kings would designate themselves as the shepherds of their peoples. Moses and David in the Old Testament, before being called to become the leaders and pastors of the People of God, were in fact shepherds with flocks.

In the anguish of the period of the Exile, confronted by the failure of Israel's shepherds, that is, of its political and religious leaders, Ezekiel sketched the image of God himself as the Shepherd of his people. Through the prophet God says: 'As a shepherd seeks out his flock . . . so will I seek out my sheep; and I will rescue them from all places where they have been scattered on a day of clouds and thick darkness' (Ez 34: 12).

---

3. Jn 10: 11-18.

Jesus now proclaims that this time has come: he himself is the Good Shepherd through whom God himself cares for his creature, man, gathering human beings and leading them to the true pasture.

St Peter, whom the Risen Lord charged to tend his sheep, to become a shepherd with him and for him, described Jesus as the *'archipoimen'* – 'Chief Shepherd' (cf. I Pt 5: 4), and by this he meant that it is only possible to be a shepherd of the flock of Jesus Christ through him and in very close communion with him.

The Sacrament of Ordination expresses this very point: through the Sacrament the priest is totally inserted into Christ, so that by starting from him and acting in his sight he may carry out in communion with him the service of Jesus, the one Shepherd, in whom God, as man, wants to be our Shepherd.

The Gospel we have heard this Sunday is only a part of Jesus' great discourse on shepherds. In this passage, the Lord tells us three things about the true shepherd: he gives his own life for his sheep; he knows them and they know him; he is at the service of unity.

Before reflecting on these three characteristics essential to shepherds, it might be useful to recall briefly the previous part of the discourse on shepherds in which Jesus, before designating himself as the Shepherd, says, to our surprise: 'I am the door' (Jn 10: 7).

It is through him that one must enter the service of shepherd. Jesus highlights very clearly this basic condition by saying: 'he who . . . climbs in by another way, that man is a thief and a robber' (Jn 10: 1). This word 'climbs' – *anabainei* in Greek – conjures up the image of someone climbing over a fence to get somewhere out of bounds to him.

'To climb' – here too we can also see the image of careerism, the attempt to 'get ahead', to gain a position through the Church: to make use of and not to serve. It is the image of a man who wants to make himself important, to become a person of note through the priesthood; the image of someone who has as his aim his own exaltation and not the humble service of Jesus Christ.

But the only legitimate ascent towards the shepherd's ministry is the Cross. This is the true way to rise; this is the true door. It is not the desire to become 'someone' for oneself, but rather to exist for others, for Christ, and thus through him and with him to be there for the people he seeks, whom he wants to lead on the path of life.

One enters the priesthood through the Sacrament, and this means precisely: through the gift of oneself to Christ, so that he can make use of me; so that I may serve him and follow his call, even if it proves contrary to my desire for self-fulfilment and esteem.

Entering by the door which is Christ means knowing and loving him more and more, so that our will may be united with his will, our action become one with his action.

Dear friends, let us pray ever anew for this intention, let us strive precisely for this: in other words, for Christ to grow within us and for our union with him to become ever deeper, so that through us it is Christ himself who tends the flock.

Let us now take a closer look at the three fundamental affirmations of Jesus on the good shepherd. The first one, which very forcefully pervades the whole discourse on shepherds, says: the shepherd lays down his life for the sheep. The mystery of the Cross is at the centre of Jesus' service as a shepherd: it is the great service that he renders to all of us.

He gives himself and not only in a distant past. In the Holy Eucharist he does so every day, he gives himself through our hands, he gives himself to us. For this good reason the Holy Eucharist, in which the sacrifice of Jesus on the Cross remains continually present, truly present among us, is rightly at the centre of priestly life.

And with this as our starting point, we also learn what celebrating the Eucharist properly means: it is an encounter with the Lord, who strips himself of his divine glory for our sake, allows himself be humiliated to the point of death on the Cross and thus gives himself to each one of us.

The daily Eucharist is very important for the priest. In it he exposes himself ever anew to this mystery; ever anew he puts himself in God's hands, experiencing at the same time the joy of knowing that He is present, receives me, ever anew raises and supports me, gives me his hand, himself. The Eucharist must become for us a school of life in which we learn to give our lives.

Life is not only given at the moment of death and not only in the manner of martyrdom. We must give it day by day. Day after day it is necessary to learn that I do not possess my life for myself. Day by day I must learn to abandon myself; to keep myself available for whatever he, the Lord, needs of me at a given moment, even if other things seem more appealing and more important to me: it means giving life, not taking it.

It is in this very way that we experience freedom: freedom from ourselves, the vastness of being. In this very way, by being useful, in being a person whom the world needs, our life becomes important and beautiful. Only those who give up their own life find it.

Secondly the Lord tells us: 'I know my own [sheep] and my own [sheep] know me, as the Father knows me and I know the Father' (Jn 10: 14-15).

Here, two apparently quite different relationships are interwoven in this phrase: the relationship between Jesus and the Father and the relationship between Jesus and the people entrusted to him. Yet both these relationships go together, for in the end people belong to the Father and are in search of the

Creator, of God.

When they realize that someone is speaking only in his own name and drawing from himself alone, they guess that he is too small and cannot be what they are seeking; but wherever another's voice re-echoes in a person, the voice of the Creator, of the Father, the door opens to the relationship for which the person is longing.

Consequently, this is how it must be in our case. First of all, in our hearts we must live the relationship with Christ and, through him, with the Father; only then can we truly understand people, only in the light of God can the depths of man be understood. Then those who are listening to us realize that we are not speaking of ourselves or of some thing, but of the true Shepherd.

Obviously, Jesus' words also contain the entire practical pastoral task, caring for men and women, going to seek them out, being open to their needs and questions.

Obviously, practical, concrete knowledge of the people entrusted to me is fundamental, and obviously, it is important to understand this way of 'knowing' others in the biblical sense: there is no true knowledge without love, without an inner relationship and deep acceptance of the other. The shepherd cannot be satisfied with knowing names and dates. His way of knowing his sheep must always also be knowing with the heart.

However, it is only possible to do this properly if the Lord has opened our hearts; if our knowing does not bind people to our own small, private self, to our own small heart, but rather makes them aware of the Heart of Jesus, the Heart of the Lord. It must be knowing with the Heart of Jesus, oriented to him, a way of knowing that does not bind the person to me but guides him or her to Jesus, thereby making one free and open. And in this way we too will become close to men and women.

Let us always pray to the Lord anew that we may be granted this way of knowing with the Heart of Jesus, of not binding to me but of binding to the Heart of Jesus and thereby creating a true community.

Lastly, the Lord speaks to us of the service of unity that is entrusted to the shepherd: 'I have other sheep that are not of this fold; I must bring them also, and they will heed my voice. So there will be one flock, one shepherd' (Jn 10: 16).

John repeated the same thing after the Sanhedrin had decided to kill Jesus, when Caiaphas said that it would be better for the people that one man die for them rather than the entire nation perish. John recognized these words of Caiaphas as prophetic, adding: 'Jesus should die for the nation, and not for the nation only, but to gather into one the children of God who are scattered abroad' (11: 52).

The relationship between the Cross and unity is revealed: the Cross is the price of unity. Above all, however, it is the universal horizon of Jesus' action that emerges.

If, in his prophecy about the shepherd, Ezekiel was aiming to restore unity among the dispersed tribes of Israel (cf. Ez 34: 22-24), here it is a question not only of the unification of a dispersed Israel but of the unification of all the children of God, of humanity – of the Church of Jews and of pagans.

Jesus' mission concerns all humanity. Therefore, the Church is given responsibility for all humanity, so that it may recognize God, the God who for all of us was made man in Jesus Christ, suffered, died and was raised.

The Church must never be satisfied with the ranks of those whom she has reached at a certain point or say that others are fine as they are: Muslims, Hindus and so forth. The Church can never retreat comfortably to within the limits of her own environment. She is charged with universal solicitude; she must be concerned with and for one and all.

We generally have to 'translate' this great task in our respective missions. Obviously, a priest, a pastor of souls, must first and foremost be concerned with those who believe and live with the Church, who seek in her their way of life and on their part, like living stones, build the Church, hence, also build and support the priest.

However, we must also – as the Lord says – go out ever anew 'to the highways and hedges' (Lk 14: 23), to deliver God's invitation to his banquet also to those who have so far heard nothing or have not been stirred within.

This universal service has many forms. One of them is also the commitment to the inner unity of the Church, so that over and above differences and limitations she may be a sign of God's presence in the world, which alone can create this unity.

Among the sculptures of her time, the ancient Church discovered the figure of a shepherd carrying a sheep across his shoulders. Such images may perhaps be part of the idyllic dream of rural life that fascinated the society of that epoch.

For Christians, however, this figure with all its naturalness became the image of the One who set out to seek his lost sheep: humanity; the image of the One who follows us even into our deserts and confusion; the image of the One who took upon his shoulders the lost sheep, which is humanity, and carried it home.

It has become the image of the true Shepherd, Jesus Christ. Let us entrust ourselves to him. We entrust you to him, dear brothers, especially at this moment, so that he may lead you and carry you all the days of your life; so that he may help you to become, through him and with him, good shepherds of his flock. Amen!

APOSTOLIC JOURNEY OF HIS HOLINESS
BENEDICT XVI TO MUNICH,
ALTÖTTING AND REGENSBURG
(9-14 SEPTEMBER, 2006)

Homily given at

MARIAN VESPERS WITH THE RELIGIOUS AND SEMINARIANS OF BAVARIA

Basilica of Saint Anne, Altötting
Monday, 11 September 2006

To be with Him and to be sent out

Here in Altötting, in this grace-filled place, we have gathered
– seminarians preparing for the priesthood, priests, men and
women religious and members of the Society for Spiritual
Vocations – gathered in the Basilica of Saint Anne, before the
shrine to her daughter, the Mother of the Lord. We have gathered
here to consider our vocation to serve Jesus Christ and, under
the watchful gaze of Saint Anne, in whose home the greatest
vocation in the history of salvation developed, to understand
it better. Mary received her vocation from the lips of an angel.
The Angel does not enter our room visibly, but the Lord has a
plan for each of us, he calls each one of us by name. Our task is
to learn how to listen, to perceive his call, to be courageous and
faithful in following him and, when all is said and done, to be

found trustworthy servants who have used well the gifts given us.

We know that the Lord seeks labourers for his harvest. He himself said as much: 'The harvest is plentiful, but the labourers are few; therefore ask the Lord of the harvest to send out labourers into his harvest' (Mt 9: 37-38). That is why we are gathered here: to make this urgent request to the Lord of the harvest. God's harvest is indeed great, and it needs labourers: in the so-called Third World – in Latin America, in Africa and in Asia – people are waiting for heralds to bring them the Gospel of peace, the good news of God who became man. But also in the so-called West, here among us in Germany, and in the vast lands of Russia it is true that a great harvest could be reaped. But there is a lack of people willing to become labourers for God's harvest. Today it is as then, when the Lord was moved with pity for the crowds which seemed like sheep without a shepherd – people who probably knew how to do many things, but found it hard to make sense of their lives. Lord, look upon our troubled times, which need preachers of the Gospel, witnesses to you, persons who can point the way towards 'life in abundance'! Look upon our world and feel pity once more! Look upon our world and send us labourers! With this petition we knock on God's door; but with the same petition the Lord is also knocking on the doors of our own heart. Lord do you want me? Is it not perhaps too big for me? Am I too small for this? 'Do not be afraid', the Angel said to Mary. 'Do not fear: I have called you by name', God says through the Prophet Isaiah (43: 1) to us – to each of us.

Where do we go, if we say 'yes' to the Lord's call? The briefest description of the priestly mission – and this is true in its own way for men and women religious too – has been given to us by the Evangelist Mark. In his account of the call of the Twelve, he says: 'Jesus appointed twelve to be with him and to be sent out'

(3: 14). To be with Jesus and, being sent, to go out to meet people – these two things belong together and together they are the heart of a vocation, of the priesthood. To be with him and to be sent out – the two are inseparable. Only one who is 'with him' comes to know him and can truly proclaim him. And anyone who has been with him cannot keep to himself what he has found; instead, he has to pass it on. Such was the case with Andrew, who told his brother Simon: 'We have found the Messiah' (Jn 1: 41). And the Evangelist adds: 'He brought Simon to Jesus' (Jn 1: 42). Pope Gregory the Great, in one of his homilies, once said that God's angels, however far afield they go on their missions, always move in God. They remain always with him. And while speaking about the angels, Saint Gregory thought also of bishops and priests: wherever they go, they should always 'be with him'. We know this from experience: whenever priests, because of their many duties, allot less and less time to being with the Lord, they eventually lose, for all their often heroic activity, the inner strength that sustains them. Their activity ends up as an empty activism. To be with Christ – how does this come about? Well, the first and most important thing for the priest is his daily Mass, always celebrated with deep interior participation. If we celebrate Mass truly as men of prayer, if we unite our words and our activities to the Word that precedes us and let them be shaped by the Eucharistic celebration, if in Communion we let ourselves truly be embraced by him and receive him – then we are being with him.

The Liturgy of the Hours is another fundamental way of being with Christ: here we pray as people conscious of our need to speak with God, while lifting up all those others who have neither the time nor the ability to pray in this way. If our Eucharistic celebration and the Liturgy of the Hours are to remain meaningful, we need to devote ourselves constantly anew to the spiritual reading of sacred Scripture; not only to be able to decipher and explain words from the distant past, but to discover the word of comfort that the Lord is now speaking to me, the Lord who challenges me by this word. Only in this way will we be capable of bringing the inspired Word to the men and women of our time as the contemporary and living Word of God.

Eucharistic adoration is an essential way of being with the Lord. Thanks to Bishop Schraml, Altötting now has a new 'treasury'. Where once the treasures of the past were kept, precious historical and religious items, there is now a place for the Church's true treasure: the permanent presence of the Lord in his Sacrament. In one of his parables the Lord speaks of a treasure hidden in the field; whoever finds it sells all he has in order to buy that field, because the hidden treasure is more valuable than anything else. The hidden treasure, the good greater than any other good, is the Kingdom of God – it is Jesus himself, the Kingdom in person. In the sacred Host, he is present, the true treasure, always waiting for us. Only by adoring this presence do we learn how to receive him properly – we learn the reality of communion, we learn the Eucharistic celebration from the inside. Here I would like to quote some fine words of Saint Edith Stein, Co-Patroness of Europe, who wrote in one of her letters: 'The Lord is present in the tabernacle in his divinity and his humanity. He is not there for himself, but for us: for it is his joy to be with us. He knows that we, being as we are, need to have him personally near. As a result, anyone with normal thoughts and feelings will naturally be drawn to spend time with him, whenever possible and as much as possible' (*Gesammelte Werke* VII, 136ff.). Let us love being with the Lord! There we can speak with him about everything. We can offer him our petitions, our concerns, our troubles. Our joys. Our gratitude, our disappointments, our needs and our aspirations. There we can also constantly ask him: 'Lord send labourers into your harvest! Help me to be a good worker in your vineyard!'

Here in this Basilica, our thoughts turn to Mary, who lived her life fully 'with Jesus' and consequently was, and continues to be, close to all men and women. The many votive plaques are a concrete sign of this. Let us think of Mary's holy mother, Saint Anne, and with her let us also think of the importance of mothers and fathers, of grandmothers and grandfathers, and the importance of the family as an environment of life and prayer, where we learn to pray and where vocations are able to develop.

Here in Altötting, we naturally think in a special way of good Brother Conrad.[4] He renounced a great inheritance because he wanted to follow Jesus Christ unreservedly and to be completely with him. As the Lord recommended in the parable, he chose to take the lowest place, that of a humble lay-brother and porter. In his porter's lodge he was able to achieve exactly what Saint Mark tells us about the Apostles: 'to stay with him', 'to be sent' to others. From his cell he could always look at the tabernacle and thus always 'stay with Christ'. From this contemplation he learned the boundless goodness with which he treated the people who would knock at his door at all hours – sometimes mischievously, in order to provoke him, at other times loudly and impatiently. To all of them, by his sheer goodness and humanity, and without grand words, he gave a message more valuable than words alone. Let us pray to Brother Saint Conrad; let us ask him to help us to keep our gaze fixed on the Lord, in order to bring God's love to the men and women of our time. Amen!

---

4. St Conrad (1818-94) spent most of his life as a Capuchin with the responsibility of being, for forty-one years, the porter at Altötting. Great devotion to the Blessed Sacrament and to Our Lady shone through his welcoming those who came to the door of the Capuchin Friary at Altötting.

CHRISM MASS

Saint Peter's Basilica
Holy Thursday, 5 April 2007

The Sacred Exchange

Leo Tolstoy, the Russian writer, tells in a short story of a harsh sovereign who asked his priests and sages to show him God so that he might see him. The wise men were unable to satisfy his desire.

Then a shepherd, who was just coming in from the fields, volunteered to take on the task of the priests and sages. From him the king learned that his eyes were not good enough to see God. Then, however, he wanted to know at least what God does. 'To be able to answer your question,' the shepherd said to the king, 'we must exchange our clothes.'

Somewhat hesitant but impelled by curiosity about the information he was expecting, the king consented; he gave the shepherd his royal robes and had himself dressed in the simple clothes of the poor man.

Then came the answer: 'This is what God does.' Indeed, the Son of God, true God from true God, shed his divine splendour: 'he emptied himself, taking the form of a servant, being born in the likeness of men; and being found in human form he humbled himself . . . , even unto death on a cross' (cf. Phil 2: 6ff.).

God, as the Fathers say, worked the *sacrum commercium*, the sacred exchange: he took on what was ours, so that we might receive what was his and become similar to God.

With regard to what happens in Baptism, St Paul explicitly uses the image of clothing: 'For as many of you as were baptized into Christ have put on Christ' (Gal 3: 27). This is what is fulfilled in Baptism: we put on Christ, he gives us his garments and these are not something external. It means that we enter into an existential communion with him, that his being and our being merge, penetrate one another.

'It is no longer I who live, but Christ who lives in me', is how Paul himself describes the event of his Baptism in his Letter to the Galatians (2: 20). Christ has put on our clothes: the pain and joy of being a man, hunger, thirst, weariness, our hopes and disappointments, our fear of death, all our apprehensions until death. And he has given to us his 'garments'.

What in the Letter to the Galatians Paul describes as a simple 'fact' of Baptism – the gift of new being – he presents to us in the Letter to the Ephesians as an ongoing task: 'Put off your old nature which belongs to your former manner of life . . . and [you must] put on the new nature, created after the likeness of God in true righteousness and holiness. Therefore, putting away falsehood, let everyone speak the truth with his neighbour, for we are members of one another. Be angry but do not sin. . .' (Eph 4: 22-26).

This theology of Baptism returns in a new way and with a new insistence in priestly Ordination. Just as in Baptism an 'exchange of clothing' is given, an exchanged destination, a new existential communion with Christ, so also in priesthood there is an exchange: in the administration of the sacraments, the priest now acts and speaks *'in persona Christi'*. In the sacred mysteries, he does not represent himself and does not speak expressing himself, but speaks for the Other, for Christ.

Thus, in the Sacraments, he dramatically renders visible what being a priest means in general; what we have expressed with our *'Adsum* – I am ready', during our consecration to the priesthood: I am here so that you may make use of me. We put ourselves at the disposal of the One who 'died for all, that those who live might live no longer for themselves. . .' (II Cor 5: 15). Putting ourselves at Christ's disposal means that we allow ourselves to be attracted within his 'for all': in being with him we can truly be 'for all'.

In persona Christi: at the moment of priestly Ordination, the Church has also made this reality of 'new clothes' visible and comprehensible to us externally through being clothed in liturgical vestments.

In this external gesture she wants to make the interior event visible to us, as well as our task which stems from it: putting on Christ; giving ourselves to him as he gave himself to us.

This event, the 'putting on of Christ', is demonstrated again and again at every Holy Mass by the putting on of liturgical vestments. Vesting ourselves in them must be more than an external event: it means entering ever anew into the 'yes' of our office – into that 'no longer I' of Baptism which Ordination to the priesthood gives to us in a new way and at the same time asks of us.

The fact that we are standing at the altar clad in liturgical vestments must make it clearly visible to those present that we are there 'in the person of an Other'. Just as in the course of time priestly vestments developed, they are a profound symbolic expression of what the priesthood means.

I would therefore like to explain to you, dear Confreres, on this Holy Thursday, the essence of the priestly ministry, interpreting the liturgical vestments themselves, which are precisely intended to illustrate what 'putting on Christ', what speaking and acting *in persona Christi*, mean.

Putting on priestly vestments was once accompanied by prayers that helped us understand better each single element of the priestly ministry.

Let us start with the amice. In the past – and in monastic orders still today – it was first placed on the head as a sort of hood, thus becoming a symbol of the discipline of the senses and of thought necessary for a proper celebration of Holy Mass. My thoughts must not wander here and there due to the anxieties and expectations of my daily life; my senses must not be attracted by what there, inside the church, might accidentally captivate the eyes and ears. My heart must open itself docilely to the Word of God and be recollected in the prayer of the Church, so that my thoughts may receive their orientation from the words of the proclamation and of prayer. And the gaze of my heart must be turned toward the Lord who is in our midst: this is what the *ars celebrandi* means: the proper way of celebrating.

If I am with the Lord, then, with my listening, speaking and acting, I will also draw people into communion with him.

The texts of the prayer expressed by the alb and the stole both move in the same direction. They call to mind the festive robes which the father gave to the prodigal son who had come home dirty, in rags.

When we approach the liturgy to act in the person of Christ, we all realize how distant we are from him; how much dirt there is in our lives. He alone can give us festive robes, can make us worthy to preside at his table, to be at his service.

Thus, the prayers also recall the words of Revelation, which say that it was not due to their own merit that the robes of the 144,000 elect were worthy of God. The Book of Revelation says that they had washed their robes in the Blood of the Lamb and thus made them white and shining like light (cf. Rv 7: 14).

When I was little, I used to ask myself about this: when one washes something in blood, it certainly does not become white! The answer is: the 'Blood of the Lamb' is the love of the Crucified Christ. It is this love that makes our dirty clothes white, that makes our clouded spirit true and bright; that transforms us, despite all our shadows, into 'light in the Lord'.

By putting on the alb we must remind ourselves: he suffered for me, too. And it is only because his love is greater than all my sins that I can represent him and witness to his light.

But with the garment of light which the Lord gave us in Baptism and in a new way in priestly Ordination, we can also think of the wedding apparel which he tells us about in the parable of God's banquet.

In the homilies of Gregory the Great, I found in this regard a noteworthy reflection. Gregory distinguishes between Luke's version of the parable and Matthew's. He is convinced that the Lucan parable speaks of the eschatological marriage feast, whereas – in his opinion – the version handed down by Matthew anticipates this nuptial banquet in the liturgy and life of the Church. In Matthew, in fact, and only in Matthew, the king comes into the crowded room to see his guests. And here in this multitude he also finds a guest who was not wearing wedding clothes, who is then thrown outside into the darkness.

Then Gregory asks himself: 'But what kind of clothes ought he to have been wearing? All those who are gathered in the Church have received the new garment of baptism and the faith; otherwise, they would not be in the Church. So what was it that was still lacking? What wedding clothes must there be in addition?'

The Pope responds: 'the clothes of love'. And unfortunately, among his guests to whom he had given new clothes, the white clothes of rebirth, the king found some who were not wearing the purple clothes of twofold love, for God and for neighbour.

'In what condition do we want to come to the feast in Heaven, if we are not wearing wedding clothes – that is, love, which alone can make us beautiful?", the Pope asks. A person without love is dark within. External shadows, of which the Gospel speaks, are only the reflection of the internal blindness of the heart (cf. *Hom.* 38, 8-13).

Now that we are preparing for the celebration of Holy Mass, we must ask ourselves whether we are wearing these clothes of love. Let us ask the Lord to keep all hostility away from our hearts, to remove from us every feeling of self-sufficiency and truly to clothe ourselves with the vestment of love, so that we may be luminous persons and not belong to darkness.

Lastly, one additional brief word on the chasuble. The traditional prayer when one puts on the chasuble sees it as representing the yoke of the Lord which is imposed upon us as priests. And it recalls the words of Jesus, who invites us to take his yoke upon us and to learn from him who is 'gentle and lowly in heart' (Mt 11: 29).

Taking the Lord's yoke upon us means first of all: learning from him. It means always being ready to go to his school. From him we must learn gentleness and meekness: the humility of God who shows himself in his being a man.

St Gregory of Nazianzus once asked himself why God wanted to become a man. The most important and for me the most moving part of his answer is: 'God wanted to realize what obedience means to us and he wanted to measure everything on the basis of his own suffering, on the originality of his love for us. In this way, he himself can directly know what it is that we feel – what is asked of us, what indulgence we deserve – calculating our weakness on the basis of his suffering' (*Orationes* 30; *Theological Talk* IV, 6).

At times we would like to say to Jesus: Lord, your yoke is far from light. Indeed, it is tremendously heavy in this world. But then looking at the One who bore everything – who tried out on himself obedience, weakness, suffering, all the darkness

– then these complaints of ours fade. His yoke is that of loving with him. And the more we love him and with him become loving people, the lighter becomes his seemingly burdensome yoke.

Let us pray to him to help us become with him people who are loving, thereby to increasingly experience how beautiful it is to take up his yoke. Amen.

MASS OF THANKSGIVING IN REMEMBRANCE OF THE POPE'S 80th BIRTHDAY

St Peter's Square
Second Sunday of Easter, 15 April 2007

A Demanding Gift

Birth and rebirth, an earthly family and the great family of God: this is the great gift of God's multiple mercies, the foundation which supports us. As I continued on my path through life, I encountered a new and demanding gift: the call to the priestly ministry.

On the Feast of Sts Peter and Paul in 1951, as I faced this task, when we were lying prostrate on the floor of the Cathedral of Freising – we were more than 40 companions – and above us all the saints were invoked, I was troubled by an awareness of the poverty of my life.

Yes, it was a consolation that the protection of God's saints, of the living and the dead, was invoked upon us. I knew that I would not be left on my own. And what faith the words of Jesus, which we heard subsequently on the lips of the bishop during the Ordination liturgy, inspire in us! 'No longer do I call you servants, but my friends. . . .' I have been able to experience this deeply: he, the Lord, is not only the Lord but also a friend. He has placed his hand upon me and will not leave me.

These words were spoken in the context of the conferral of the faculty for the administration of the Sacrament of Reconciliation and thus, in Christ's Name, to forgive sins. We heard the same thing in today's Gospel: the Lord breathes upon his disciples. He grants them his Spirit – the Holy Spirit: 'If you forgive the sins of any, they are forgiven. . . .'

The Spirit of Jesus Christ is the power of forgiveness. He is the power of Divine Mercy. He makes it possible to start all over again – ever anew. The friendship of Jesus Christ is the friendship of the One who makes us people who forgive, the One who also forgives us, raises us ceaselessly from our weakness and in this very way educates us, instils in us an awareness of the inner duty of love, of the duty to respond with our faithfulness to his trust.

In the Gospel passage for today we also heard the story of the Apostle Thomas' encounter with the Risen Lord: the Apostle is permitted to touch his wounds and thereby recognizes him – over and above the human identity of Jesus of Nazareth, Thomas recognizes him in his true and deepest identity: 'My Lord and my God!' (Jn 20: 28).

The Lord took his wounds with him to eternity. He is a wounded God; he let himself be injured through his love for us. His wounds are a sign for us that he understands and allows himself to be wounded out of love for us.

These wounds of his: how tangible they are to us in the history of our time! Indeed, time and again he allows himself to be wounded for our sake. What certainty of his mercy, what consolation do his wounds mean for us! And what security they give us regarding his identity: 'My Lord and my God!' And what a duty they are for us, the duty to allow ourselves in turn to be wounded for him!

God's mercy accompanies us daily. To be able to perceive his mercy it suffices to have a heart that is alert. We are excessively inclined to notice only the daily effort that has been imposed upon us as children of Adam.

If, however, we open our hearts, then as well as immersing ourselves in them we can be constantly aware of how good God is to us; how he thinks of us precisely in little things, thus helping us to achieve important ones.

With the increasing burden of responsibility, the Lord has also brought new assistance to my life. I repeatedly see with grateful joy how large is the multitude of those who support me with their prayers; I see that with their faith and love they help me carry out my ministry; I see that they are indulgent with my shortcomings and also recognize in Peter's shadow the beneficial light of Jesus Christ.

At this moment, therefore, I would like to thank the Lord and all of you with all my heart. I wish to end this Homily with a prayer of the holy Pope, St Leo the Great, that prayer which precisely 30 years ago I had written on the souvenir cards for my episcopal ordination:

'Pray to our good God that in our day he will be so good as to reinforce faith, multiply love and increase peace. May he render me, his poor servant, adequate for his task and useful for your edification, and grant me to carry out this service so that together with the time given to me my dedication may grow, Amen.'

From the Homily given at the

ORDINATION OF NEW PRIESTS FOR THE DIOCESE OF ROME

St Peter's Basilica
Fourth Sunday of Easter, 29 April 2007

'Sharers in the very mission of Christ'

Jesus speaks of himself as the Good Shepherd who gives eternal life to his sheep (cf. Jn 10: 28). This image of the shepherd is deeply rooted in the Old Testament and dear to Christian tradition. The Prophets attributed to David the title: 'Shepherd of Israel', which hence possesses an indisputable messianic importance (cf. Ex 34: 23).

Jesus is the true Shepherd of Israel, since he is the Son of Man who desired to share the condition of human beings to give them new life and lead them to salvation.

Significantly, the Evangelist adds to the term *'shepherd'* the adjective *kalós,* good, which he only uses with reference to Jesus and his mission. In the account of the Wedding at Cana, the adjective *kalós* is also used twice to signify the wine offered by Jesus, and it is easy to see it as a symbol of the *good* wine of messianic times (cf. 2: 10).

'I give them (that is, to my sheep) eternal life and they shall never perish' (Jn 10: 28). These are the words of Jesus, who had said a little earlier, 'the good shepherd lays down his life for his sheep' (cf. Jn 10: 11).

John uses the verb *tithénai – to offer,* which he repeats in the following verses (cf. 15, 17, 18). We find the same verb in the Last Supper narrative when Jesus 'laid aside his garments' in order to 'take' them back later (cf. Jn 13: 4, 12).

Thus, it is clear that the intention is to affirm that the Redeemer has absolute freedom to do with his life as he chooses and thereby give it up or take it back freely.

Christ is the true Good Shepherd who gave his life for his sheep, for us, sacrificing himself on the Cross. He knows his sheep and his sheep know him, just as the Father knows him and he knows the Father (cf. Jn 10: 14-15).

This is not a matter of mere intellectual knowledge but of a profound, personal relationship: a knowledge of the heart, of one who loves and one who is loved; of one who is faithful and one who knows how to be trustworthy.

It is a knowledge of love, by virtue of which the Pastor invites his sheep to follow him and which is fully manifest in the gift of eternal life that he offers to them (cf. Jn 10: 27-28).

Dear Ordinands, may the certainty that Christ does not abandon us and that no obstacle can prevent the accomplishment of his universal plan of salvation be a cause of constant con-solation – also in difficulties – and steadfast hope for you. The Lord's goodness is always with you, and it is powerful.

The Sacrament of Orders, which you are about to receive, will make you sharers in the very mission of Christ; you will be called to scatter the seed of his Word, the seed that carries in itself the Kingdom of God; to dispense divine mercy and to nourish the faithful at the table of his Body and Blood.

To be his worthy ministers, you must ceaselessly nourish yourselves with the Eucharist, source and summit of Christian life.

In approaching the altar, your daily school of holiness, of communion with Jesus, of the way of entering into his sentiments in order to renew the sacrifice of the Cross, you will increasingly discover the richness and tenderness of the love of the divine Teacher, who today is calling you to a closer friendship with him.

If you listen docilely to him, if you follow him faithfully, you will learn to express in your life and in your pastoral ministry his love and his passion for the salvation of souls.

With Jesus' help, dear Ordinands, each one of you will become a Good Shepherd, ready, if necessary, to lay down your life for him.

Thus it was at the beginning of Christianity with the first disciples while, as we heard in the First Reading,[5] the Gospel continued to be disseminated amid consolations and difficulties.

It is worth stressing the last words in the passage from the Acts of the Apostles which we have heard: 'The disciples were filled with joy and with the Holy Spirit' (13: 52).

Despite the misunderstandings and disagreements, about which we have heard, the apostle of Christ does not lose joy; indeed, he is a witness of that joy which flows from being with the Lord and from love for him and for the brothers and sisters.

On today's World Day of Prayer for Vocations, whose theme this year is: '*The vocation to the service of the Church as communion*', let us pray that all who are chosen to such a lofty mission may be accompanied by the prayerful communion of all the faithful.

Let us pray that in every parish and Christian community attention to vocations and to the formation of priests will increase: it begins in the family, continues at the seminary and involves all who have at heart the salvation of souls.

Dear brothers and sisters who are taking part in this evocative celebration, and in the first place you, relatives, family members

---

5. Acts 13: 43-52.

and friends of these 22 deacons who will shortly be ordained priests!

Let us surround these brothers of ours in the Lord with our spiritual solidarity. Let us pray that they may be faithful to the mission to which the Lord is calling them today and ready to renew their 'yes' to God, their 'here I am', every day without reserve.

And let us ask the Lord of the harvest on this Day for Vocations to continue to bring forth many holy priests who are totally dedicated to the service of the Christian people.

At this most solemn and important moment of your life, dear Ordinands, I once again address you with affection. On this day Jesus repeats to you: 'I no longer call you servants, but friends'. Welcome and nurture this divine friendship with 'Eucharistic love'!

May Mary, the heavenly Mother of priests, accompany you. May she who beneath the Cross united herself with the Sacrifice of her Son and after the Resurrection accepted together with the other disciples the gift of the Spirit, help you and each one of us, dear brothers in the priesthood, to allow ourselves to be inwardly transformed by God's grace.

Only in this way is it possible to be faithful images of the Good Shepherd; only in this way can we carry out joyfully the mission of knowing, guiding and loving the flock which Jesus acquired at the price of his blood. Amen.

Homily given at

THE CHRISM MASS

Saint Peter's Basilica
Holy Thursday, 20 March 2008

'To stand in your presence and serve you'

Every year the Chrism Mass exhorts us to enter into that 'yes' to God's call, which we pronounced on the day of our priestly ordination. '*Adsum* – here I am!', we have said like Isaiah, when he heard God's voice asking: 'Whom shall I send, and who will go for us?' 'Here am I! Send me', Isaiah responded (Is 6: 8). Then the Lord himself, through the hands of the bishop, placed his hands on us and we gave ourselves to his mission. Subsequently, we have followed many ways in the range of his call. Can we always affirm what Paul wrote to the Corinthians after years of Gospel service, often marked by fatigue and suffering of every type: 'Our zeal has not slackened in this ministry which has been entrusted to us by God's mercy' (cf. II Cor 4: 1)? 'Our zeal has not slackened'. Let us pray on this day that it may always be kindled anew, that it may be ever nourished by the living flame of the Gospel.

At the same time Holy Thursday is an occasion for us to ask ourselves over and over again: to what did we say our 'yes'? What does this 'being a priest of Jesus Christ' mean? The Second Canon of our Missal, which was probably compiled in Rome already at the end of the second century, describes the essence of the priestly ministry with the words with which, in the Book of Deuteronomy (18: 5, 7), the essence of the Old Testament priesthood is described: *astare coram te et tibi ministrare* ['to stand and minister in the name of the Lord']. There are therefore two duties that define the essence of the priestly ministry: in the first place, 'to stand in his [the Lord's] presence'. In the Book of Deuteronomy this is read in the context of the preceding disposition, according to which priests do not receive any portion of land in the Holy Land – they live of God and for God. They did not attend to the usual work necessary to sustain daily life. Their profession was to 'stand in the Lord's presence' – to look to him, to be there for him. Hence, ultimately, the word indicated a life in God's presence, and with this also a ministry of representing others. As the others cultivated the land, from which the priest also lived, so he kept the world open to God, he had to live with his gaze on him. Now if this word is found in the Canon of the Mass immediately after the consecration of the gifts, after the entrance of the Lord in the assembly of prayer, then for us this points to being before the Lord present, that is, it indicates the Eucharist as the centre of priestly life. But here too, the meaning is deeper. During Lent the hymn that introduces the Office of Readings of the Liturgy of the Hours – the Office that monks once recited during the night vigil before God and for humanity – one of the duties of Lent is described with the imperative: *arctius perstemus in custodia* – we must be even more intensely alert. In the tradition of Syrian monasticism, monks were qualified as 'those who remained standing'. This standing was an expression of vigilance. What was considered here as a duty of the monks, we can rightly see also as an expression of the priestly mission and as a correct interpretation of the word of Deuteronomy: the priest must be on the watch. He must be on his guard in the face of the imminent powers of evil. He must keep the world awake for God. He must be the one who remains standing: upright before the trends of time. Upright in truth. Upright in the commitment for good. Being before the Lord must always also include, at its depths, responsibility for humanity to the Lord, who in his turn takes on the burden of all of us to the Father. And it must be a taking on of him, of Christ, of his word, his truth, his love. The priest must be upright, fearless and prepared to sustain even offences for the Lord, as referred to in the Acts of the Apostles: they were 'rejoicing that they were counted worthy to suffer dishonour for the name' (5: 41) of Jesus.

Now let us move on to the second word that the Second Canon repeats from the Old Testament text – 'to stand in your presence and serve you'. The priest must be an upright person, vigilant, a person who remains standing. Service is then added to all this. In the Old Testament text this word has an essentially ritualistic meaning: all acts of worship foreseen by the Law are the priests' duty. But this action, according to the rite, was classified as service, as a duty of service, and thus it explains in what spirit this activity must take place. With the assumption of the word 'serve' in the Canon, the liturgical meaning of this term was adopted in a certain way – to conform with the novelty of the Christian cult. What the priest does at that moment, in the Eucharistic celebration, is to serve, to fulfil a service to God and a service to humanity. The cult that Christ rendered to the Father was the giving of himself to the end for humanity. Into this cult, this service, the priest must insert himself. Thus, the word 'serve' contains many dimensions. In the first place, part of it is certainly the correct celebration of the liturgy and of the sacraments in general, accomplished through interior participation. We must learn to increasingly understand the sacred liturgy in all its essence, to develop a living familiarity with it, so that it becomes the soul of our daily life. It is then that we celebrate in the correct way; it is then that the *ars celebrandi,* the art of celebrating, emerges by itself. In this art there must be nothing artificial. If the liturgy is the central duty of the priest, this also means that prayer must be a primary reality, to be learned ever anew and ever more deeply at the school of Christ and of the Saints of all the ages. Since the Christian liturgy by its nature is also always a proclamation, we must be people who are familiar with the Word of God, love it and live by it: only then can we explain it in an adequate way. 'To serve the Lord' – priestly service precisely also means to learn to know the Lord in his Word and to make it known to all those he entrusts to us.

Lastly, two other aspects are part of service. No one is closer to his master than the servant who has access to the most private dimensions of his life. In this sense 'to serve' means closeness, it requires familiarity. This familiarity also bears a danger: when we continually encounter the sacred it risks becoming habitual for us. In this way, reverential fear is extinguished. Conditioned by all our habits we no longer perceive the great, new and surprising fact that he himself is present, speaks to us, gives himself to us. We must ceaselessly struggle against this becoming accustomed to the extraordinary reality, against the indifference of the heart, always recognizing our insufficiency anew and the grace that there is in the fact that he consigned himself into our hands. To serve means to draw near, but above all it also means obedience. The servant is under the word: 'not my will, but thine, be done' (Lk 22: 42). With this word Jesus, in the Garden of Olives, has resolved the decisive battle against sin, against the rebellion of the sinful heart. Adam's sin consisted precisely in the fact that he wanted to accomplish his own will and not God's. Humanity's temptation is always to want to be totally autonomous, to follow its own will alone and to maintain that only in this way will we be free; that only thanks to a similarly unlimited freedom would man be completely man. But this is precisely how we pit ourselves against the truth. Because the truth is that we must share our freedom with others and we can be free only in communion with them. This shared freedom can be true freedom only if we enter into what constitutes the very measure of freedom, if we enter into God's will. This fundamental obedience that is part of the human being – a person cannot be merely for and by himself – becomes still more concrete in the priest: we do not preach ourselves, but him and his Word, which we could not have invented ourselves. We proclaim the Word of Christ in the correct way only in communion with his Body. Our obedience is a believing with the Church, a thinking and speaking with the Church, serving through her. What Jesus predicted to Peter also always applies: 'You will be taken where you do not want to go'. This letting oneself be guided where one does not want to be led is an essential dimension of our service, and it is exactly what makes us free. In this being guided, which can be contrary to our ideas and plans, we experience something new – the wealth of God's love.

'To stand in his presence and serve him': Jesus Christ as the true High Priest of the world has conferred to these words a previously unimaginable depth. He, who as Son was and is the Lord, has willed to become that Servant of God which the vision of the Book of the Prophet Isaiah had foreseen. He has willed to be the Servant of all. He has portrayed the whole of his high priesthood in the gesture of the washing of the feet. With the gesture of love to the end he washes our dirty feet, with the humility of his service he purifies us from the illness of our pride. Thus, he makes us able to become partakers of God's banquet. He has descended, and the true ascent of man is now accomplished in our descending with him and toward him. His elevation is the Cross. It is the deepest descent and, as love pushed to the end, it is at the same time the culmination of the ascent, the true 'elevation' of humanity. 'To stand in his presence and serve him': this now means to enter into his call to serve God. The Eucharist as the presence of the descent and ascent of Christ thus always recalls, beyond itself, the many ways of service through love of neighbour. Let us ask the Lord on this day for the gift to be able to say again in this sense our 'yes' to his call: 'Here am I! Send me' (Is 6: 8). Amen.

Homily given at the

ORDINATION OF NEW PRIESTS FOR THE DIOCESE OF ROME

St Peter's Basilica
Sixth Sunday of Easter, 27 April 2008

'If you love me'

Today the words that say 'You have brought them abundant joy and great rejoicing' come true for us in a very special way. Indeed, besides the joy of celebrating the Eucharist on the Lord's Day there is the spiritual exultation of the Easter Season, of which we have now reached the Sixth Sunday, and above all the celebration of the ordination of new priests. Together with you I greet with affection the 29 deacons who are shortly to be ordained priests. I express deep gratitude to those who have guided them in their process of discernment and preparation and I ask you all to thank God for his gift to the Church of these new priests. Let us support them with intense prayer during this celebration, in a spirit of fervent praise to the Father who has called them, to the Son who has attracted them to him and to the Spirit who has formed them. The ordination of new priests usually takes place on the Fourth Sunday of Easter, known as 'Good Shepherd' Sunday, which is also the World Day of Prayer for Vocations but this was not possible because I was away on the Pastoral Visit to the United States of America. The image of the Good Shepherd seems to be the one which sheds more light than any other on the role and ministry of the priest in the Christian community. However, the biblical passages which today's liturgy offers for our meditation also illumine the priest's mission, from a different angle.

The First Reading, from chapter 8 of the Acts of the Apostles, tells of the mission of the deacon Philip in Samaria. I would like immediately to draw attention to the sentence that ends the first part of the text: 'The rejoicing in that town rose to fever pitch' (v. 8). This expression does not communicate an idea or a theological concept but refers to a circumstantiated event, something that changed people's lives: in a specific city of Samaria, in the period that followed the violent persecution of the Church in Jerusalem (cf. Acts 8: 1), something happened that caused 'great joy'. So what was it? The sacred Author recounts that to escape the persecution which had been unleashed in Jerusalem against those who had converted to Christianity, all the disciples except the Apostles left the Holy City and scattered in the countryside around it. This distressing event mysteriously and providentially gave new dynamism to the spread of the Gospel. Among those who had dispersed was Philip, one of the Community's seven deacons, a deacon like you, dear Ordinands although, of course, in a different way because, in the unrepeatable season of the nascent Church, the Apostles and deacons were endowed by the Holy Spirit with extraordinary power in both preaching and in healing. Now, it happened that the inhabitants of the region of Samaria mentioned in this chapter of the Acts of the Apostles unanimously accepted Philip's proclamation and, thanks to their adherence to the Gospel, he was able to heal many sick people. In that town of Samaria, in the midst of a people traditionally despised and virtually excommunicated by the Jews, the proclamation of Christ, which opened the hearts of all who accepted it, resounded. This explains why, St Luke emphasizes, 'there was great joy' in that town.

Dear friends, this is also your mission: to bring the Gospel to everyone so that everyone may experience the joy of Christ and that there be joy in every city. What can be more beautiful than this? What can be greater, more exciting, than cooperating in spreading the Word of life in the world, than communicating the living water of the Holy Spirit? To proclaim and to witness joy: this is the central core of your mission, dear deacons who will soon become priests. The Apostle Paul called Gospel ministers 'servants of joy'. He wrote in his Second Letter to the Christians of Corinth: 'Domineering over your faith is not my purpose. I prefer to work with you toward your happiness. As regards faith, you are standing firm' (II Cor 1: 24). These are programmatic words for every priest. In order to be collaborators in the joy of others, in a world that is often sad and negative, the fire of the Gospel must burn within you and the joy of the Lord dwell in you. Only then will you be able to be messengers and multipliers of this joy, bringing it to all, especially to those who are sorrowful and disheartened.

Let us return to the First Reading which offers us another element of meditation. In it is mentioned a prayer meeting which takes place precisely in the Samarian town evangelized by the deacon Philip. Presiding at it are the Apostles Peter and John, two 'pillars' of the Church, who came from Jerusalem to visit this new community and strengthen it in the faith. Through the imposition of their hands, the Holy Spirit descended upon all those who had been baptized. In this episode we can see a first attestation of the rite of 'Confirmation', the second Sacrament of Christian initiation. The reference to the ritual gesture of the imposition of hands is especially meaningful also for us who are gathered here. Indeed, it is also the central gesture of the rite of Ordination through which, in a little while, I shall confer on the candidates the dignity of the priesthood. It is a sign inseparable from the prayer of which it is a silent prolongation. Without speaking, the consecrating bishop and after him the other priests, place their hands on the heads of the ordinands, thereby expressing the invocation to God that he will pour out his Spirit upon them and transform them, making them sharers in the priesthood of Christ. It is a matter of only a few seconds, a very short time, but full of an extraordinary spiritual intensity.

Dear Ordinands, in the future you must always think back to this moment, to this gesture that has nothing magical about it and yet is full of mystery, because this is the origin of your new mission. In that silent prayer the encounter between two freedoms comes into being: the freedom of God, who works through the Holy Spirit and the freedom of man. The imposition of hands visually expresses the specific manner of this meeting: the Church, in the person of the bishop standing with extended hands, prays to the Holy Spirit to consecrate the candidate: the deacon, on his knees, receives the imposition of hands and entrusts himself to this mediation. Altogether these gestures are important but the invisible spiritual movement that they express is infinitely more important, a movement clearly evoked by the sacred silence that envelops everything, internal and external.

We also find in this Gospel passage the mysterious Trinitarian 'movement' that leads the Holy Spirit and the Son to dwell in the disciples. Here, it is Jesus himself who promises that he will ask the Father to send his Spirit, defined as 'another Paraclete' (Jn 14: 16), a Greek word that is equivalent to the Latin *advocatus*, an advocate-defender. The first Paraclete is in fact the Incarnate Son who came to defend man from the accuser by antonomasia, who is Satan. At the moment when Christ, his mission fulfilled, returns to the Father, he sends the Spirit as Defender and Consoler to remain with believers for ever, dwelling within them. Thus, through the mediation of the Son and of the Holy Spirit, an intimate relationship of reciprocity is established between God the Father and the disciples: 'I am in my Father, and you in me, and I in you', Jesus says (Jn 14: 20). However, all this depends on one condition which Christ imposes clearly at the beginning: 'If you love me' (Jn 14: 15), and which he repeats at the end: 'He who obeys the commandments he has from me is the man who loves me; and he who loves me will be loved by my Father. I too will love him and reveal myself to him' (Jn 14: 21). Without love for Jesus, which is expressed in the observance of his commandments, the person is excluded from the Trinitarian movement and begins to withdraw into himself, losing the ability to receive and to communicate God.

'If you love me'. Dear friends, Jesus said these words at the Last Supper in the context of the moment when he instituted the Eucharist and the priesthood. Although they were addressed to the Apostles, in a certain sense they are addressed to all their successors and to priests who are the closest collaborators of the successors of the Apostles. Let us hear them again today as an invitation to live our vocation in the Church ever more coherently: you, dear Ordinands, listen to them with special emotion because precisely today Christ makes you share in his priesthood. Accept them with faith and with love! Let them be imprinted on your hearts, let them accompany you on the journey of your whole life. Do not forget them, do not lose them on the way! Reread them, meditate on them often and, especially, pray on them. Thus you will remain faithful to Christ's love and realize with joy ever new that his divine word 'walks' with you and 'grows' within you.

One more observation on the Second Reading: it is taken from the First Letter of Peter, near whose tomb we find ourselves and to whose intercession I would especially like to entrust you. I make my own and consign to you with affection his words: 'Venerate the Lord, that is, Christ, in your hearts. Should anyone ask you the reason for this hope of yours, be ever ready to reply' (3: 15). Worship Christ the Lord in your hearts: cultivate a personal relationship of love with him, your first and greatest love, one and totalizing, in which to live, purify, illumine and sanctify all your other relationships. The 'hope that is in you' is linked to this 'adoration', to this love of Christ, who through the Spirit, as we said, dwells within us. Our hope, your hope is God, in Jesus and in the Spirit. It is a hope which from today becomes in you a 'priestly hope', that of Jesus the Good Shepherd who dwells within you and gives shape to your desires in accordance with his divine Heart: a hope of life and forgiveness for the people who will be entrusted to your pastoral care; a hope of holiness and apostolic fruitfulness for yourselves and for all the Church; a hope of openness to faith and to the encounter with God for those who support you in their quest for the truth; a hope of peace and comfort for the suffering and for those wounded by life.

Dear friends, this is my wish on this day which is so important for you: that hope rooted in faith may become more and more your own! And may you, who are wise and generous, gentle and strong, always be respectful and convinced witnesses and dispensers of it. May the Virgin Mary, whom I urge you to welcome anew, as did the Apostle John beneath the Cross, accompany you on this mission and protect you always, as the Mother and Star of your life and your priesthood. Amen!

APOSTOLIC JOURNEY OF HIS HOLINESS
BENEDICT XVI TO FRANCE ON THE
OCCASION OF THE 150th ANNIVERSARY
OF THE APPARITIONS OF THE BLESSED
VIRGIN MARY AT LOURDES
(12-15 SEPTEMBER, 2008)

From the Homily given at the

CELEBRATION OF VESPERS
WITH PRIESTS, RELIGIOUS,
SEMINARIANS AND DEACONS

Notre-Dame Cathedral, Paris
Friday, 12 September 2008

Instruments of the Holy Spirit

'Unless the Lord builds the house, those who build it labour in vain' (Ps 126:1). Who is this Lord, if not our Lord Jesus Christ? It is he who founded his Church and built it on rock, on the faith of the Apostle Peter. In the words of Saint Augustine, 'It is Jesus Christ our Lord who himself builds his temple. Many indeed labour to build, yet unless the Lord intervenes to build, in vain do the builders labour' (*Tract. in Ps.* 126:2). Dear friends, Augustine goes on to ask how we can know who these builders are, and his answer is this: 'All those who preach God's word in the Church, all who are ministers of God's divine Sacraments. All of us run, all of us work, all of us build', yet it is God alone who, within us, 'builds, exhorts, and inspires awe; who opens our understanding and guides our minds to faith' (ibid.). What marvels surround our work in the service of God's word! We are instruments of the Holy Spirit; God is so humble that he uses us to spread his word. We become his voice, once we have listened carefully to the word coming from his mouth. We place his word on our lips in order to bring it to the world. He accepts the offering of our prayer and through it he communicates himself to everyone we meet. Truly, as Paul tells the Ephesians, 'he has blessed us in Christ with every spiritual blessing' (1: 3), for he has chosen us to be his witnesses to the ends of the earth, and he made us his elect, even before we came into existence, by a mysterious gift of his grace.

God's Word, the Eternal Word, who was with him from the beginning (cf. Jn 1:1), was born of a woman, born a subject of the law, in order to redeem the subjects of the law, 'to redeem those who were under the law, so that we might receive adoption as sons' (cf. Gal 4:4-5). The Son of God took flesh in the womb of a woman, a virgin. Your cathedral is a living hymn of stone and light in praise of that act, unique in the annals of human history: the eternal Word of God entering our history in the fullness of time to redeem us by his self-offering in the sacrifice of the Cross. Our earthly liturgies, entirely ordered to the celebration of this unique act within history, will never fully express its infinite meaning. Certainly, the beauty of our celebrations can never be sufficiently cultivated, fostered and refined, for nothing can be too beautiful for God, who is himself infinite Beauty. Yet our earthly liturgies will never be more than a pale reflection of the liturgy celebrated in the Jerusalem on high, the goal of our pilgrimage on earth. May our own celebrations nonetheless resemble that liturgy as closely as possible and grant us a foretaste of it!

Even now the word of God is given to us as the soul of our apostolate, the soul of our priestly life. Each morning the word awakens us. Each morning the Lord himself 'opens our ear' (cf. Is 50:5) through the psalms in the Office of Readings and Morning Prayer. Throughout the day, the word of God becomes the substance of the prayer of the whole Church, as she bears witness in this way to her fidelity to Christ. In the celebrated phrase of Saint Jerome: 'Ignorance of the Scriptures is ignorance of Christ' (*Prol. in Is.*). Dear brother priests, do not be afraid to spend much time reading and meditating on the Scriptures and praying the Divine Office! Almost without your knowing it, God's word, read and pondered in the Church, acts upon you and transforms you. As the manifestation of divine Wisdom, if that word becomes your life 'companion', it will be your 'good counsellor' and an 'encouragement in cares and grief' (Wis 8: 9).

'The word of God is living and active, sharper than any two-edged sword', as the author of the Letter to the Hebrews tells us (4:12). Dear seminarians, who are preparing to receive the sacrament of Holy Orders and thus to share in the threefold office of teaching, governing and sanctifying, this word is given to you as a precious treasure. By meditating on it daily, you will enter into the very life of Christ which you will be called to radiate all around you. By his word, the Lord Jesus instituted the Holy Sacrament of his Body and Blood; by his word, he healed the sick, cast out demons and forgave sins; by his word, he revealed to us the hidden mysteries of his Kingdom. You are called to become stewards of this word which accomplishes what it communicates. Always cultivate a thirst for the word of God! Thus you will learn to love everyone you meet along life's journey. In the Church everyone has a place, everyone! Every person can and must find a place in her.

And you, dear deacons, effective co-workers of the bishops and priests, continue to love the word of God! You proclaim the Gospel at the heart of the Eucharistic celebration, and you expound it in the catechesis you offer to your brothers and sisters. Make the Gospel the centre of your lives, of your service to your neighbours, of your entire *diakonia*. Without seeking to take the place of priests, but assisting them with your friendship and your activity, may you be living witnesses to the infinite power of God's word!

In a particular way, men and women religious and all consecrated persons draw life from the Wisdom of God expressed in his word. The profession of the evangelical counsels has configured you, dear consecrated persons, to Christ, who for our sakes became poor, obedient and chaste. Your only treasure – which, to tell the truth, will alone survive the passage of time and the curtain of death – is the word of the Lord. It is he who said: 'Heaven and earth will pass away; my words will not pass away' (Mt 24:35). Your obedience is, etymologically, a 'hearing', for the word *obey* comes from the Latin *obaudire*, meaning to turn one's ear to someone or something. In obeying, you turn your soul towards the one who is the Way, and the Truth and the Life (cf. Jn 14:6), and who says to you, as Saint Benedict taught his monks: 'Hear, my child, the teaching of the Master, and hearken to it with all your heart' (prologue to the *Rule of Saint Benedict)*. Finally, let yourselves be purified daily by him who said: 'Every branch that bears fruit my Father prunes, to make it bear more fruit' (Jn 15: 2). The purity of God's word is the model for your own chastity, ensuring its spiritual fruitfulness.

Dear brothers and sisters, in Our Lady we have the finest example of fidelity to God's word. Her great fidelity found fulfilment in the Incarnation; with absolute confidence, Mary can say: 'Behold the handmaid of the Lord; let it be done to me according to your word!' (Lk 1: 38). Our evening prayer is about to take up the Magnificat, the song of her whom all generations will call blessed. Mary believed in the fulfilment of the words the Lord had spoken to her (cf. Lk 1: 45); she hoped against all hope in the resurrection of her Son; and so great was her love for humanity that she was given to us as our Mother (cf. Jn 19: 27). Thus we see that 'Mary is completely at home with the word of God; with ease she moves in and out of it. She speaks and thinks with the word of God; the word of God becomes her word, and her word issues from the word of God' (*Deus Caritas Est*, 41). To her, then, we can say with confidence: 'Holy Mary, Mother of God, our Mother, teach us to believe, to hope, to love with you. Show us the way to his Kingdom!' (*Spe Salvi*, 50). Amen.

APOSTOLIC JOURNEY OF HIS HOLINESS BENEDICT XVI TO FRANCE ON THE OCCASION OF THE 150th ANNIVERSARY OF THE APPARITIONS OF THE BLESSED VIRGIN MARY AT LOURDES (12-15 SEPTEMBER, 2008)

From the Homily given at

HOLY MASS

Notre-Dame, Esplanade des Invalides, Paris
Saturday, 13 September 2008

'For the salvation of the world'

How do we reach God? How do we manage to discover or rediscover him whom man seeks at the deepest core of himself, even though he so often forgets him? Saint Paul asks us to make use not only of our reason, but above all our faith in order to discover him. Now, what does faith say to us? The bread that we break is a communion with the Body of Christ. The cup of blessing which we bless is a communion with the Blood of Christ. This extraordinary revelation comes to us from Christ and has been transmitted to us by the Apostles and by the whole Church for almost two thousand years: Christ instituted the sacrament of the Eucharist on the evening of Holy Thursday. He wanted his sacrifice to be presented anew, in an unbloody manner, every time a priest repeats the words of consecration over the bread and wine. Millions of times over the last twenty centuries, in the humblest chapels and in the most magnificent basilicas and cathedrals, the risen Lord has given himself to his people, thus becoming, in the famous expression of Saint Augustine, 'more intimate to us than we are to ourselves' (cf. *Confessions,* III, 6, 11).

Brothers and sisters, let us give the greatest veneration to the sacrament of the Body and Blood of the Lord, the Blessed Sacrament of the real presence of the Lord to his Church and to all humanity. Let us take every opportunity to show him our respect and our love! Let us give him the greatest marks of honour! Through our words, our silences, and our gestures, let us never allow our faith in the risen Christ, present in the Eucharist, to lose its savour in us or around us! As Saint John Chrysostom said magnificently, 'Let us behold the ineffable generosity of God and all the good things that he enables us to enjoy, when we offer him this cup, when we receive communion, thanking him for having delivered the human race from error, for having brought close to him those who were far away, for having made, out of those who were without hope and without God in the world, a people of brothers, fellow heirs with the Son of God' (Homily 24 on the First Letter to the Corinthians, 1). 'In fact', he continues, 'what is in the cup is precisely what flowed from his side, and it is of this that we partake' (ibid.). There is not only partaking and sharing, there is 'union', says the Doctor whose name means 'golden mouth'.

The Mass is the sacrifice of thanksgiving par excellence, the one which allows us to unite our own thanksgiving to that of the Saviour, the Eternal Son of the Father. It also makes its own appeal to us to shun idols, for, as Saint Paul insists, 'you cannot partake of the table of the Lord and the table of demons' (1 Cor 10: 21). The Mass invites us to discern what, in ourselves, is obedient to the Spirit of God and what, in ourselves, is attuned to the spirit of evil. In the Mass, we want to belong only to Christ and we take up with gratitude – with thanksgiving – the cry of the psalmist: 'How shall I repay the Lord for his goodness to me?' (Ps 116: 12). Yes, how can I give thanks to the Lord for the life he has given me? The answer to the psalmist's question is found in the psalm itself, since the word of God responds graciously to its own questions. How else could we render thanks to the Lord for all his goodness to us if not by attending to his own words: 'I will raise the cup of salvation, I will call on the name of the Lord' (Ps 116: 13)?

To raise the cup of salvation and call on the name of the Lord, is that not the very best way of 'shunning idols', as Saint Paul asks us to do? Every time the Mass is celebrated, every time Christ makes himself sacramentally present in his Church, the work of our salvation is accomplished. Hence to celebrate the Eucharist means to recognize that God alone has the power to grant us the fullness of joy and teach us true values, eternal values that will never pass away. God is present on the altar, but he is also present on the altar of our heart when, as we receive Communion, we receive him in the sacrament of the Eucharist. He alone teaches us to shun idols, the illusions of our minds.

Now, dear brothers and sisters, who can raise the cup of salvation and call on the name of the Lord in the name of the entire people of God, except the priest, ordained for this purpose by his bishop? At this point, allow me to issue an appeal, confident in the faith and generosity of the young people who are considering a religious or priestly vocation: do not be afraid! Do not be afraid to give your life to Christ! Nothing will ever replace the ministry of priests at the heart of the Church! Nothing will ever replace a Mass for the salvation of the world! Dear young and not so young who are listening to me, do not leave Christ's call unanswered. Saint John Chrysostom, in his *Treatise on the Priesthood*, showed how sluggish man could be in responding, but he is nonetheless the living example of God's action at the heart of a human freedom that allows itself to be shaped by his grace.

May God our Father bring you to himself and cause the splendour of his glory to shine upon you! May the only Son of God, our master and brother, reveal to you the beauty of his risen face! May the Holy Spirit fill you with his gifts and grant you the joy of knowing the peace and light of the Most Holy Trinity, now and for ever! Amen!

II.
ADDRESSES

From an

ADDRESS TO THE CLERGY OF ROME

Basilica of St John Lateran
Friday, 13 May 2005

Rooted in Christ

Dear priests, the quality of your lives and your pastoral service seem to indicate that in this Diocese, as in many others of the world, we have now left behind us that period of identity crisis that troubled so many priests. However, still present are the causes of the 'spiritual wilderness' that afflict humanity in our day and consequently also undermine the Church, which dwells among humankind. How can we not fear that they may also ensnare the lives of priests?

It is indispensable, therefore, to return ever anew to the solid root of our priesthood. This root, as we well know, is one: Jesus Christ our Lord. It is he whom the Father sent, he is the cornerstone (cf. I Pt 2: 7). Through him, through the mystery of his death and Resurrection, the Kingdom of God is established and the salvation of the human race brought about.

This Jesus, however, possesses nothing of his own; everything he has is from the Father and for the Father. So he says that his doctrine is not his own but comes from the One who sent him (cf. Jn 7: 16): and that he, the Son, cannot do anything by himself (cf. Jn 5: 19, 30).

Dear friends, this is also the true nature of our priesthood. In fact, all that constitutes our priestly ministry cannot be the product of our personal abilities. This is true for the administration of the Sacraments, but it is also true for the service of the Word: we are not sent to proclaim ourselves or our personal opinions, but the mystery of Christ and, in him, the measure of true humanism. We are not charged to utter many words, but to echo and bear the message of a single 'Word', the Word of God made flesh for our salvation. Consequently, these words of Jesus also apply to us: 'My doctrine is not my own; it comes from him who sent me' (Jn 7: 16).

Dear priests of Rome, the Lord calls us friends, he makes us his friends, he entrusts himself to us, he entrusts to us his Body in the Eucharist, he entrusts to us his Church. Therefore, we must be true friends to him, we must have the same perception as he has, we must want what he wants and not what he does not want. Jesus himself tells us: 'You are my friends if you do what I command you' (Jn 15: 14). Let this be our common resolution: all of us together, to do his holy will, in which lies our freedom and our joy.

Since the priesthood is rooted in Christ, it is by its nature in the Church and for the Church. Indeed, the Christian faith is not something purely spiritual and internal, nor is our relationship with Christ itself exclusively subjective and private.

Rather, it is a completely concrete and ecclesial relationship. At times, the ministerial priesthood has a constitutive relationship with the Body of Christ in his dual and inseparable dimensions as Eucharist and as Church, as Eucharistic body and Ecclesial body.

Therefore, our ministry is *amoris officium* (St Augustine, *In Iohannis Evangelium Tractatus* 123, 5),[6] it is the office of the Good Shepherd who offers his life for his sheep (cf. Jn 10: 14-15). In

------

6. *A duty of love.*

the Eucharistic mystery, Christ gives himself ever anew, and it is precisely in the Eucharist that we learn love of Christ, hence, love for the Church.

I therefore repeat with you, dear brothers in the priesthood, the unforgettable words of John Paul II: 'Holy Mass is the absolute centre of my life and of every day of my life' (*Address at a Symposium in honour of the 30th anniversary of the Decree 'Presbyterorum Ordinis'*, 27 October 1995, n. 4; *L'Osservatore Romano* English edition, 15 November 1995, p. 7). And each one of us should be able to say these words are his own: Holy Mass is the absolute centre of my life and of my every day.

Likewise, obedience to Christ, who made amends for Adam's disobedience, is in practice expressed in ecclesial obedience, which for the priest in daily life means first and foremost obedience to his bishop. In the Church, however, obedience is not something formalistic; it is obedience to the one who, in turn, obeys and personifies the obedient Christ. All this neither frustrates nor even attenuates the practical requirements of obedience, but guarantees theological depth and its Catholic tone: in the bishop we obey Christ and the whole Church which he represents in this place.

Jesus Christ was sent by the Father, through the power of the Holy Spirit, for the salvation of the entire human family, and we priests are enabled through the grace of the sacrament to share in this mission of his. As the Apostle Paul writes, 'God . . . has given us the ministry of reconciliation. . . . This makes us ambassadors for Christ, God as it were appealing through us. We implore you, in Christ's name: be reconciled to God' (II Cor 5: 18-29). This is how St Paul describes our mission as priests.

Therefore, in the homily prior to the Conclave, I spoke of the 'holy restlessness' that must animate us, the concern to bring to everyone the gift of faith, to offer everyone the salvation that alone endures for ever. And in a city as large as Rome, which on the one hand is so steeped in faith yet in which so many people live who have not really perceived in their hearts the proclamation of faith, we should be especially impelled by this restless concern to bring this joy, this centre of life, which gives it meaning and direction.

Dear brother priests of Rome, the Risen Christ is calling us to be his witnesses and gives us the strength of his Spirit to enable us to be truly such. It is necessary, therefore, to be with him (cf. Mk 3: 14; Acts 1: 21-23) for life. As in the first description of the 'munus apostolicum'[7] in Mark 3, an account is given of what the Lord thought being an apostle should mean: being with him and being available for the mission. The two things go together and only by staying with him are we also and always on the move with the Gospel towards others.

Thus, it is essential to be with him, and in this way that restlessness pervades us and enables us to bring the power and joy of the faith to others with our whole lives and not only with just a few words.

The Apostle Paul's words can apply to us: 'Yet preaching the Gospel is not the subject of a boast; I am under compulsion and have no choice. I am ruined if I do not preach it! . . . Although I am not bound to anyone, I made myself the slave of all so as to win over as many as possible. . . . I have made myself all things to all men in order to save at least some of them' (I Cor 9: 16-22).

These words that are the self-portrait of the Apostle are also the portrait of every priest. Making oneself 'all things to all men' is expressed in daily life, in attention to every person and family: in this regard, you priests of Rome have a great tradition, and I say so with deep conviction, and you are also honouring it today when the city has spread so much and is profoundly changed. It

---

7. *Apostolic office.*

is crucial, as you well know, that the closeness and attention to everyone are always expressed in Christ's Name and constantly strive to lead people to him.

This closeness and dedication, of course, has a personal cost for each one of you, for us. It involves time, worry, the expenditure of energy. I am aware of your daily efforts and want to thank you on behalf of the Lord. But I also want to help you as much as I can so that you do not yield under this burden.

To be able to bear, indeed, even to grow, as persons and as priests, it is fundamental first of all to have intimate communion with Christ, whose food was to do the will of his Father (cf. Jn 4: 34): all we do is done in communion with him, and we thus rediscover ever anew the unity of our lives in the many facets of our daily occupations.

Let us also learn from the Lord Jesus Christ, who sacrificed himself to do the will of the Father, the art of priestly ascesis which is also necessary today: it should not be exercised on a par with pastoral activities as an additional burden that makes our day even more difficult. On the contrary, we must learn how to surpass ourselves, how to give and how to offer our lives.

But, if all this is truly to happen within us so that our very action may truly become our ascesis and our self-giving, so that all this may not be just a wish, there is no doubt that we need moments in which to replenish our energies, including the physical, and especially to pray and meditate, returning to our inner selves and finding the Lord within us.

Thus, spending time in God's presence in prayer is a real pastoral priority; it is not an addition to pastoral work: being before the Lord is a pastoral priority and in the final analysis, the most important. John Paul II showed this to us in the most practical and enlightened way in every circumstance of his life and ministry.

Dear priests, we can never sufficiently emphasize how

fundamental and crucial our personal response to the call to holiness is. It is not only the condition for our personal apostolate to be fruitful but also, and more generally, for the face of the Church to reflect the light of Christ (cf. *Lumen Gentium*, n. 1), thereby inducing people to recognize and adore the Lord.

We must first inwardly accept the Apostle Paul's plea that we let ourselves be reconciled to God (cf. II Cor 5: 20), asking the Lord with a sincere heart and courageous determination to take away from us all that separates us from God and is contrary to the mission we have received. The Lord is merciful, we are certain, and will answer our prayer.

Having listened to comments from the Roman Clergy,
Pope Benedict responded:

The priest, deacon, catechist and Religious must, on the one hand, proclaim, be witnesses. But naturally, for this they must listen, in a two-fold sense: on the one hand, with their soul open to Christ, interiorly listening to his Word so that it is assimilated and transformed and forms my being; and on the other, listening to today's humanity, our neighbours, those of my parish, those for whom I have been given a certain responsibility.

Naturally, listening to the world of today that exists also in us, we listen to all the problems, all the difficulties that are contrary to faith. And we must be able to seriously take upon ourselves these problems.

In his First Letter, St Peter, the first Bishop of Rome, says that we Christians must be ready to explain our faith. This presupposes that we ourselves have understood the reason of faith, that we have truly 'digested', even rationally, with the heart, with the wisdom of heart, this word that can truly be an answer for others.

In the First Letter of St Peter, in the Greek text, with a fine play on words, it is written: 'apologia', the answer to the 'logos', of the reason for our faith. And so, the 'logos', the reason for the faith, the word of faith, must become the answer of faith. And we know well that the language of faith is often very far from today's men and women; it can bring them close only if it becomes in us our modern-day language. We are contemporary, we live in this world, with these thoughts, these emotions. If it is transformed in us, one can find the answer.

Naturally, I am aware and we all know that many are not immediately able to identify themselves with, to understand, to assimilate all that the Church teaches. It seems to me important firstly to awaken this intention to believe with the Church, even if personally someone may not yet have assimilated many particulars. It is necessary to have this will to believe with the Church, to have trust that this Church – the community not only of 2,000 years of pilgrimage of the people of God, but the community that embraces heaven and earth, the community where all the righteous of all times are therefore present – that this Church enlivened by the Holy Spirit truly carries within the 'compass' of the Spirit and therefore is the true subject of faith.

The individual, then, is inserted into this subject, adheres to it, and so, even if he or she is still not completely penetrated by this, the person has trust and participates in the faith of the Church, wants to believe with the Church. To me, this seems like our lifelong pilgrimage: to arrive with our thought, our affections, with our entire life at the communion of faith. We can offer this to everyone, so that little by little one can identify and especially take this step over and over again to trust in the faith of the Church, to insert themselves in this pilgrimage of faith, so as to receive the light of faith.

To conclude, I would like once more to say 'thank you' for the contribution expressed here regarding Christocentrism, the requirement for our faith to be ever nourished by personal encounter with Christ, a personal friendship with Jesus.[8]

Romano Guardini correctly said 70 years ago that the essence of Christianity is not an idea but a Person. Great theologians have tried to describe the essential ideas that make up Christianity. But in the end, the Christianity that they constructed was not convincing, because Christianity is in the first place an Event, a Person. And thus in the Person we discover the richness of what is contained. This is important.

8. The 'contribution' referred to by Pope Benedict XVI was given during the comments that he listened to after the first part of his address.

AN ADDRESS TO THE DIOCESAN CLERGY OF AOSTA

Parish Church at Introd (Aosta Valley)
Monday, 25 July 2005

Sowers of the Word

I would first like to express my joy and gratitude for this opportunity to meet you. As Pope, one risks being somewhat distant from real, everyday life and especially from the priests who work on the front line in so many parishes in this very Valley, and now, as His Excellency said, with the lack of vocations, also in particularly demanding conditions of physical commitment.[9]

It is therefore a grace for me to be able to meet the priests and presbyterate of this Valley in this beautiful church. And I would like to say 'thank you' for coming; for you too, it is the vacation period.

To see you gathered together and thus to see myself united with you, being close to the priests who work day after day for the Lord as sowers of the Word, is a comfort and joy to me.

Last week, two or three times, it seems to me, we heard this Parable of the Sower, which was formerly a parable of consolation in a situation different from ours but in a certain sense also similar.

The Lord's work had begun with great enthusiasm. The sick were visibly cured, everyone listened joyfully to the statement:

---

9. 'His Excellency' refers to the Bishop of Aosta, Mgr Giuseppe Anfossi.

'The Kingdom of God is at hand'. It really seemed that the changing of the world and the coming of the Kingdom of God would be approaching; that at last, the sorrow of the People of God would be changed into joy. People were expecting a messenger of God whom they supposed would take the helm of history in his hand. But they then saw that the sick were indeed cured, devils were expelled, the Gospel was proclaimed, but the world stayed as it was. Nothing changed. The Romans still dominated it. Life was difficult every day, despite these signs, these beautiful words. Thus, their enthusiasm was extinguished, and in the end, as we know from the sixth chapter of John, disciples also abandoned this Preacher who was preaching but did not change the world.

'What is this message? What does this Prophet of God bring?', everyone finally wondered. The Lord talks of the sower who sowed in the field of the world and the seed seemed like his Word, like those healings, a really tiny thing in comparison with historical and political reality. Just as the seed is tiny and can be ignored, so can the Word.

Yet, he says, the future is present in the seed because the seed carries within it the bread of the future, the life of the future. The seed appears to be almost nothing, yet the seed is the presence of the future, it is a promise already present today. And so, with this parable, he is saying: 'We are living in the period of the sowing, the Word of God seems but a word, almost nothing. But take heart, this Word carries life within it! And it bears fruit!' The Parable also says that much of the seed did not bear fruit because it fell on the path, on patches of rock and so forth. But the part that fell on the rich soil bore a yield of thirty- or sixty- or a hundredfold.

This enables us to understand that we too must be courageous, even if the Word of God, the Kingdom of God, seems to have no historical or political importance. In the end, on Palm Sunday

Jesus summed up, as it were, all of these teachings on the seed of the word: If the grain of wheat does not fall into the ground and die it remains single, if it falls into the earth and dies it produces an abundance of fruit. In this way he made people realize that he himself was the grain of wheat that fell into the earth and died. In the Crucifixion, everything seems to have failed, but precisely in this way, falling into the earth and dying, on the Way of the Cross, it bore fruit for each epoch, for every epoch. Here we have both the Christological interpretation, according to which Christ himself is the seed, he is the Kingdom present, and the Eucharistic dimension: this grain of wheat falls into the earth and thus the new Bread grows, the Bread of future life, the Blessed Eucharist that nourishes us and is open to the divine mysteries for new life.

It seems to me that in the Church's history, these questions that truly torment us are constantly cropping up in various forms: what should we do? People seem to have no need of us, everything we do seems pointless. Yet we learn from the Word of the Lord that this seed alone transforms the earth ever anew and opens it to true life.

I would like, as far as I can, to respond briefly to your words, Your Excellency; but I would also like to say that the Pope is not an oracle, he is infallible on the rarest of occasions, as we know. I therefore share with you these questions, these queries. I also suffer. However, let us, on the one hand, suffer all together for these problems, and let us also suffer in transforming the problems; for suffering itself is the way to transformation, and without suffering nothing is transformed.

This is also what the Parable of the Grain of Wheat that fell into the earth means: only in a process of suffering transformation does the fruit mature and the solution become clear. And if we did not suffer, the apparent ineffectiveness of our preaching would be a sign of the lack of faith, of true commitment. We must take these difficulties of our time to heart and transform them, suffering with Christ, and thereby transform ourselves. And to the extent to which we ourselves are transformed, we will also be able to respond to the question asked above, we will also be able to see the presence of the Kingdom of God and to make others see it.

The first point is a problem that exists throughout the Western world: the lack of vocations. In these past few weeks I have received *ad limina* visits from the bishops of Sri Lanka and from the southern part of Africa. Vocations there are increasing; indeed, they are so numerous that it is proving impossible to build enough seminaries to accommodate all these young men who want to be priests.

Of course, this joy also carries with it a certain sadness, since at least a part of them comes in the hope of social advancement. By becoming priests, they become like tribal chiefs, they are naturally privileged, they have a different lifestyle, etc. Therefore, weeds and wheat grow together in this beautiful crop of vocations and the bishops must be very careful in their discernment; they must not merely be content with having many future priests but must see which really are the true vocations, discerning between the weeds and the good wheat.

However, there is a certain enthusiasm of faith because they are in a specific period of history, that is, in the period in which it is clear that the traditional religions are no longer adequate. People are realizing, they are seeing that these traditional religions contain a promise within them but are waiting for something. They are awaiting a new response that purifies and, let us say, takes on all that is beautiful, setting it free from these inadequate and negative aspects. In this time of transition, in which their culture is truly reaching out to a new time in history, the two offerings – Christianity and Islam – are the possible historical responses.

Consequently, in a certain sense there is a springtime of the faith in those countries but, of course, in the context of rivalry between these two responses and also especially in the context of suffering because of the sects, who present themselves, as it were, as a Christian response that is better, easier and more accommodating. So it is that even in the history of a promise, in a springtime moment, the commitment of the one who must sow the Word with Christ and, as we say, build the Church, continues to be difficult.

The situation is different in the Western world, which is a world weary of its own culture. It is a world that has reached the time when there is no longer any evidence of the need for God, let alone Christ, and when it therefore seems that humans could build themselves on their own. In this atmosphere of a rationalism closing in on itself and that regards the model of the sciences as the only model of knowledge, everything else is subjective. Christian life too, of course, becomes a choice that is subjective, hence, arbitrary and no longer the path of life. It therefore naturally becomes difficult to believe, and if it is difficult to believe it is even more difficult to offer one's life to the Lord to be his servant.

This is certainly a form of suffering which, I would say, fits into our time in history, and in which we generally see that the so-called 'great' Churches seem to be dying. This is true particularly in Australia, also in Europe, but not so much in the United States.

On the other hand, the sects that present themselves with the certainty of a minimum of faith are growing, and the human being seeks certainty. Thus, the great Churches, especially the great traditional Protestant Churches, are truly finding themselves in a very deep crisis. The sects have the upper hand because they appear with a few simple certainties and say: 'This suffices'.

The plight of the Catholic Church is not as bad as that of the great Protestant Churches of history, but of course, she shares the problem of our historical period. I do not think that there is any system for making a rapid change. We must go on, we must go through this tunnel, this underpass, patiently, in the certainty that Christ is the answer and that in the end, his light will appear once more.

Thus, the first answer is patience, in the certainty that the world cannot live without God, the God of Revelation – and not just any god: we see how dangerous a cruel god, an untrue god can be – the God who showed us his Face in Jesus Christ. This Face of the One who suffered for us, this loving Face of the One who transforms the world in the manner of the grain of wheat that fell into the earth.

Therefore, we ourselves have this very deep certainty that Christ is the answer and that without the real God, the God with the Face of Christ, the world destroys itself; and there is growing evidence that a closed rationalism, which thinks that human beings can rebuild the world better on their own, is not true. On the contrary, without the restraint of the true God, human beings destroy themselves. We see this with our own eyes.

We ourselves must have a renewed certainty: he is the Truth; only by walking in his footsteps do we go in the right direction, and it is in this direction that we must walk and lead others.

The first point of my answer is: in all this suffering, not only should we keep our certainty that Christ really is the Face of God, but we should also deepen this certainty and the joy of knowing it and thus truly be ministers of the future of the world, of the future of every person. We should deepen this certainty in a personal relationship with the Lord because certainty can also grow with rational considerations. A sincere reflection that is also rationally convincing but becomes personal, strong and demanding by virtue of a friendship lived personally, every day, with Christ, truly seems to me to be very important.

Certainty, consequently, demands this personalization of our faith, of our friendship with the Lord, and thus new vocations also grow. We see it in the new generations after the great crisis of this cultural struggle unleashed in 1968, when the historical epoch of Christianity truly seemed to be over. We see that the promises of 1968 have not been kept and, let us say, the awareness that another way exists which is more complex because it requires this transformation of our hearts but is truer, and thus new vocations are also born. And we ourselves must also find the creativity to help young people to discover this way in the future, too. This was also evident in the dialogue with the African bishops. Despite the number of priests, many are condemned to a terrible loneliness and many do not survive morally.

And it is therefore important to live in the reality of the presbyterate, of the community of priests who help one another, who are journeying on together with solidarity in their common faith. This also seems to me to be important, for if young people see priests who are very lonely, sad and tired, they will think: 'If this is my future, then it is not for me.' A real communion of life that shows young people: 'Yes, this can be a future for me too, it is possible to live like this', must be created.

I have gone on too long. It seems to me that I have said something on the second point, even if only on part of it. It is true: to the people, especially world leaders, the Church appears as something antiquated and our proposals seem unnecessary. People behave as though they were able to and wanted to live without our words, and they always think they have no need of us. They do not seek our words.

This is true and causes us pain, but it is also part of this historical situation of a certain anthropological vision which claims that the human being must act as Karl Marx said: 'The Church has had 1,800 years to show that it could change the world and has not done anything; we will now do it on our own.'

This is a very widespread idea and is also supported by philosophers. Thus, we understand the impression of so many that it is possible to live without the Church, which appears as a vestige of the past. But it is becoming ever clearer that only moral values and strong convictions, and sacrifices, make it possible to live and to build the world. It is impossible to construct it in a mechanical way, as Karl Marx proposed, with the theories concerning capital and ownership, etc.

If there is no moral force in souls, if there is no readiness to suffer for these values, a better world is not built; indeed, on the contrary, the world deteriorates every day, selfishness dominates and destroys all. On perceiving this the question arises anew: but where does the strength come from that enables us to suffer for good too, to suffer for good that hurts me first, which has no immediate usefulness? Where are the resources, the sources? From where does the strength come to preserve these values?

It can be seen that morality as such does not survive and is not effective unless it is deeply rooted in convictions that truly provide certainty and the strength to suffer for – at the same time, they are part of love – a love that grows in suffering and is the substance of life. In the end, in fact, love alone enables us to live, and love is always also suffering: it matures in suffering and provides the strength to suffer for good without taking oneself into account at the actual moment.

It seems to me that this awareness is growing because we are already seeing the effects of a condition in which the strength that comes from a love that is the substance of my life and gives me the power to carry on the struggle for good does not exist. Here too, of course, we are in need of patience, but also an active patience in the sense of making people understand: 'You need this.'

Even if they do not convert straightaway, at least they draw closer to the circle of those in the Church who possess this inner strength. The Church has always recognized this inwardly strong group that truly has the strength of faith and of persons who are, as it were, attached to one another, moving ahead, and so participate.

I am thinking of the Lord's Parable of the Mustard Seed which was so small and then became a tree so great that the birds of the sky build their nests in it. And I should say that these birds could be the people who are not yet converted but who at least perch on the tree of the Church. I have pondered on this: in the time of the Enlightenment, the time when faith was divided between Catholics and Protestants, people believed it was necessary to preserve the common moral values by giving them a firm foundation. They thought, 'We must make the moral values independent of the religious denominations so that they can prevail *"etsi Deus non daretur"*.'[10]

Today, we are in an opposite situation; the situation has been reversed. There is no longer any proof of moral values. They become evident only if God exists. I have therefore suggested that lay people, the so-called laity, should think about whether the contrary might not be true for them today: We must live *'quasi Deus daretur'*,[11] and even if we are not strong enough to believe, we must live on this hypothesis, otherwise the world will not function; and this, it seems to me, would be a first step to approaching faith. I also see in so many contacts that, thanks be to God, dialogue with at least part of the secular world is increasing.

The third point: the plight of priests who have become scarce,

---

10. *As if God did not exist* – that is, living without the working hypothesis of God's existence.
11. *As if God exists.*

who must work in as many as three, four and at times even five parishes and are exhausted. I think that the bishop, together with his priests, is trying to discover what the best solution might be. When I was Archbishop of Munich they created this type of service solely for the Liturgy of the Word without a priest in order, let us say, to keep the community present in its own church. And they said: 'Every community should stay put and wherever there is no priest let us celebrate this Liturgy of the Word.'

The French found the Word suitable for these Sunday Assemblies 'in the absence of a priest', but after a while they realized that this could go wrong because the meaning of the Sacrament is lost, a 'Protestantization' occurs and, in the end, if it is only the Word, I can celebrate it myself in my own home.

I remember when I was a professor at Tübingen, there was the great exegete Kelemann – I do not know if you are familiar with his name – a pupil of Bultmann, who was a great theologian. Although he was a convinced Protestant, he never went to church. He used to say: 'I can also meditate at home on the Sacred Scriptures.'

The French have transformed somewhat this formula of Sunday Assemblies 'in the absence of a priest' into 'awaiting the priest'. That is, the priest must be expected, and I would say that the Liturgy of the Word should normally be an exception on Sundays, because the Lord wants to come corporally. Consequently, this must not be the solution.

Sunday was created because the Lord was raised and entered the community of the Apostles to be with them. And thus, they also understood that Saturday was no longer the liturgical day, but Sunday, on which the Lord wants to be with us physically again and again, and wants to nourish us with his Body, so that we ourselves may become his Body in the world.

We should find a way to offer many people of good will this

possibility: for now I do not presume to give formulas. I always said in Munich, but I am unacquainted with the situation here which is bound to be a little different, that our people are incredibly mobile and flexible. The young travel 50 kilometres or more to go to a discothèque, why can they also not travel 50 kilometres to go to a common church? Yet, this is something very positive and practical and I do not dare to offer formulas. However, an effort should be made to give people this sentiment: 'I need to be with the Church, to be with the living Church and with the Lord!'

PASTORAL VISIT OF HIS HOLINESS POPE BENEDICT XVI TO POLAND

AN ADDRESS GIVEN AT A MEETING WITH THE CLERGY

Warsaw Cathedral, 25 May 2006

Stand firm in the Faith

'First, I thank my God through Jesus Christ for all of you. . . . For I long to see you, that I may impart to you some spiritual gift to strengthen you, that is, that we may be mutually encouraged by each other's faith, both yours and mine' (Rom 1: 8-12).

Dear priests, I address to you these words of the Apostle Paul, because they perfectly reflect my feelings and thoughts today, my wishes and my prayers. I greet in particular Cardinal Józef Glemp, Archbishop of Warsaw and Primate of Poland, to whom I extend my most cordial congratulations on his fiftieth anniversary of priestly ordination this very day. I have come to Poland, the beloved homeland of my great Predecessor Pope John Paul II, in order to inhale, as he used to do, this atmosphere of faith in which you live, and to 'convey to you some spiritual gift so that you may be strengthened by it.' I am confident that my pilgrimage during these days will 'encourage the faith that we share, both yours and mine.'

I am meeting you today in the great Cathedral of Warsaw, every stone of which speaks of the tragic history of your capital and your country. How many trials you have endured in the recent past! We call to mind heroic witnesses to the faith, who gave their lives to God and to their fellow human beings, both canonized saints and ordinary people who persevered in rectitude, authenticity and goodness, never giving way to despair. In this cathedral I recall particularly the Servant of God Cardinal Stefan Wyszyński, whom you call 'the Primate of the Millennium'. Abandoning himself to Christ and to his Mother, he knew how to serve the Church faithfully, despite the tragic and prolonged trials that surrounded him. Let us remember with appreciation and gratitude those who did not let themselves be overwhelmed by the forces of darkness, and let us learn from them the courage to be consistent and constant in our adherence to the Gospel of Christ.

Today I am meeting you, priests called by Christ to serve him in the new millennium. You have been chosen from among the people, appointed to act in relation to God, to offer gifts and sacrifices for sins. Believe in the power of your priesthood! By virtue of the sacrament, you have received all that you are. When you utter the words 'I' and 'my' ('I absolve you' . . . 'This is my body. . .'), you do it not in your own name, but in the name of Christ, *in persona Christi*, who wants to use your lips and your hands, your spirit of sacrifice and your talent. At the moment of your ordination, through the liturgical sign of the imposition of hands, Christ took you under his special protection; you are concealed under his hands and in his Heart. Immerse yourselves in his love, and give him your love! When your hands were anointed with oil, the sign of the Holy Spirit, they were destined to serve the Lord as his own hands in today's world. They can no longer serve selfish purposes, but must continue in the world the witness of his love.

The greatness of Christ's priesthood can make us tremble. We can be tempted to cry out with Peter: 'Lord, depart from me, for I am a sinful man' (Lk 5: 8), because we find it hard to believe that Christ called us specifically. Could he not have chosen someone else, more capable, more holy? But Jesus has looked lovingly upon each one of us, and in this gaze of his we may have confidence. Let us not be consumed with haste, as if time dedicated to Christ in silent prayer were time wasted. On the contrary, it is precisely then that the most wonderful fruits of pastoral service come to birth. There is no need to be discouraged on account of the fact that prayer requires effort, or because of the impression that Jesus remains silent. He is indeed silent, but he is at work. In this regard, I am pleased to recall my experience last year in Cologne. I witnessed then a deep, unforgettable silence of a million young people at the moment of the Adoration of the Blessed Sacrament! That prayerful silence united us, it gave us great consolation. In a world where there is so much noise, so much bewilderment, there is a need for silent adoration of Jesus concealed in the Host. Be assiduous in the prayer of adoration and teach it to the faithful. It is a source of comfort and light particularly to those who are suffering.

The faithful expect only one thing from priests: that they be specialists in promoting the encounter between man and God. The priest is not asked to be an expert in economics, construction or politics. He is expected to be an expert in the spiritual life. With this end in view, when a young priest takes his first steps, he needs to be able to refer to an experienced teacher who will help him not to lose his way among the many ideas put forward by the culture of the moment. In the face of the temptations of relativism or the permissive society, there is absolutely no need for the priest to know all the latest, changing currents of thought; what the faithful expect from him is that he be a witness to the eternal wisdom contained in the revealed word. Solicitude for the quality of personal prayer and for good theological formation bear fruit in life. Living under the influence of totalitarianism may have given rise to an unconscious tendency to hide under an external mask, and in consequence to become somewhat hypocritical. Clearly this does not promote authentic fraternal relations and may lead to an exaggerated concentration on oneself. In reality, we grow in affective maturity when our hearts adhere to God. Christ needs priests who are mature, virile, capable of cultivating an authentic spiritual paternity. For this to happen, priests need to be honest with themselves, open with their spiritual director and trusting in divine mercy.

On the occasion of the Great Jubilee, Pope John Paul II frequently exhorted Christians to do penance for infidelities of the past. We believe that the Church is holy, but that there are sinners among her members. We need to reject the desire to identify only with those who are sinless. How could the Church have excluded sinners from her ranks? It is for their salvation that Jesus took flesh, died and rose again. We must therefore learn to live Christian penance with sincerity. By practising it, we confess individual sins in union with others, before them and before God. Yet we must guard against the arrogant claim of setting ourselves up to judge earlier generations, who lived in different times and different circumstances. Humble sincerity is needed in order not to deny the sins of the past, and at the same time not to indulge in facile accusations in the absence of real evidence or without regard for the different preconceptions of the time. Moreover, the *confessio peccati*,[12] to use an expression of Saint Augustine, must always be accompanied by the *confessio laudis* – the confession of praise. As we ask pardon for the wrong that was done in the past, we must also remember the good accomplished with the help of divine grace which, even if contained in earthenware vessels, has borne fruit that is often excellent.

Today the Church in Poland faces an enormous pastoral challenge: how to care for the faithful who have left the country.

---

12. *Confession of sins.*

The scourge of unemployment obliges many people to go abroad. It is a widespread and large-scale phenomenon. When families are divided in this way, when social links are broken, the Church cannot remain indifferent. Those who leave must be cared for by priests who, in partnership with the local Churches, take on a pastoral ministry among the emigrants. The Church in Poland has already given many priests and religious sisters who serve not only the Polish diaspora but also, and sometimes in extremely difficult circumstances, the missions in Africa, Asia, Latin America and other regions. Do not forget these missionaries, my dear priests. The gift of many vocations, with which God has blessed your Church, must be received in a truly Catholic perspective. Polish priests, do not be afraid to leave your secure and familiar world, to go and serve in places where priests are lacking and where your generosity can bear abundant fruit.

Stand firm in your faith! To you too I entrust this motto of my pilgrimage. Be authentic in your life and your ministry. Gazing upon Christ, live a modest life, in solidarity with the faithful to whom you have been sent. Serve everyone; be accessible in the parishes and in the confessionals, accompany the new movements and associations, support families, do not forget the link with young people, remember the poor and the abandoned. If you live by faith, the Holy Spirit will suggest to you what you must say and how you must serve. You will always be able to count on the help of her who goes before the Church in faith. I exhort you to call upon her always in words that you know well: 'We are close to you, we remember you, we watch.'

My Blessing upon all of you!

From the

MEETING WITH THE PRIESTS OF THE DIOCESE OF ALBANO

Swiss Hall at the Papal Summer Residence,
Castel Gandolfo
Thursday, 31 August 2006

Fr Giuseppe Zane, a priest 83 years old addressed Pope Benedict:

Our Bishop, if briefly, has described to you the situation of our Diocese of Albano. We priests are fully integrated into this Church and experience all the relative problems and complexities. Young and old, we all feel inadequate. This is firstly because we are so few in comparison with the many needs and we come from different backgrounds; we also suffer from a shortage of priestly vocations. That is why we sometimes feel discouraged. We try to patch things up here and there and are often forced to attend only to emergencies, without any precise projects. Seeing how much there is to do, we are tempted to give priority to 'doing' and to neglect 'being'; this is inevitably reflected in our spiritual life, our conversation with God, our prayer and our charity (love) for our brethren, especially those who are far away. Holy Father, what can you tell us about this? I am a certain age . . . but is it possible for these young confreres of mine to hope?

Pope Benedict XVI: I have no claim to be, as it were, an 'oracle' that could respond adequately to every question. St Gregory the Great's words . . . , which everyone knows, 'infirmitatem suam', also apply to the Pope. Day after day, the Pope too must know and recognize 'infirmitatem suam', his shortcomings. He must recognize that only in collaboration with everyone, in dialogue, in common cooperation, in faith as 'cooperatores veritatis'[13] – of the Truth that is a Person, Jesus – can we carry out our service together, each one doing his share. This means that my answers will not be exhaustive but piecemeal. Yet, let us agree that actually it is only in unison that we can piece together the 'mosaic' of a pastoral work that responds to the immense challenges.

Each one of us has moments of discouragement in the face of all that needs to be done, and the limits of what, instead, can realistically be done. Once again, this also concerns the Pope. What must I do at this time for the Church, with so many problems, so many joys, so many challenges that concern the universal Church? So many things happen, day after day, and I am unable to respond to them all. I do my part, I do all I can. I try to identify the priorities. And I am glad that I have so many good collaborators to help me. . . . And only with this network of collaboration, fitting myself and my own limited capacities into a broader reality, can I and dare I move ahead.

Therefore, naturally, a parish priest who is on his own sees even better that so many things still need to be done in this situation which you, Fr Zane, have briefly described. And he can only do something to 'patch things up', as you said, a kind of 'first-aid' operation, knowing that far more ought to be done.

I would say, then, that firstly, what is necessary for all of us is to recognize our own limitations, to humbly recognize that we have to leave most things to the Lord. Today, we heard in the Gospel the Parable of the Faithful Servant (Mt 24: 42-51). This servant, the Lord tells us, gives food to the others at the proper time. He does not do everything at once but is a wise and prudent servant

---

13. *Co-workers of the truth.* This was Joseph Ratzinger's episcopal motto before being elevated to the See of Peter and is drawn from III John 8.

who knows what needs to be done in a specific situation. He does so humbly, and is also sure of his master's trust. So it is that we must likewise do our utmost to be wise and prudent and to trust in the goodness of our 'Master', the Lord, for in the end it is he himself who must take the helm of his Church. We fit into her with our small gift and do the best we can, especially those things that are always necessary: celebrating the sacraments, preaching the Word, giving signs of our charity and our love.

As for the inner life you mentioned, I would say that it is essential to our service as priests. The time we set aside for prayer is not time taken from our pastoral responsibility but is precisely pastoral 'work'; it is also praying for others. In the 'Common of Pastors', one reads as a typical feature of the good pastor that *'multum oravit pro fratribus'.*[14] This is proper to the pastor, that he should be a man of prayer, that he should come before the Lord praying for others, even replacing others who perhaps do not know how to pray, do not want to pray or do not make the time to pray. Thus, it is obvious that this dialogue with God is pastoral work!

I would say further that the Church gives us, imposes upon us – but always like a good Mother – the obligation to make free time for God with the two practices that constitute a part of our duties: the celebration of Holy Mass and the recitation of the Breviary. However, rather than reciting it, this means putting it into practice by listening to the word which the Lord offers us in the Liturgy of the Hours.

It is essential to interiorize this word, to be attentive to what the Lord is saying to me with this word, to listen, then, to the comments of the Fathers of the Church or also of the Council in the Second Reading of the Office of Readings, and to pray with this great invocation, the Psalms, by which we are inserted into

14. *He prayed much on behalf of his brothers.*

the prayer of all the ages. The people of the Old Covenant pray with us, and we pray with them. We pray with the Lord, who is the true subject of the Psalms. We pray with the Church of all times. I would say that this time dedicated to the Liturgy of the Hours is precious time. The Church offers to us this freedom, this free space of life with God, which is also life for others.

Thus, it seems important to me to see that these two realities – Holy Mass truly celebrated in conversation with God and the Liturgy of the Hours – are areas of freedom, of inner life, an enrichment which the Church bestows upon us. In them, as I said, we do not only find the Church of all the ages but also the Lord himself, who speaks to us and awaits our answer. We thus learn to pray by immersing ourselves in the prayer of all times, and we also encounter the people. Let us think of the Psalms, of the words of the Prophets, of the words of the Lord and of the Apostles, let us think of the Fathers' comments.

Today, we have had St Columban's marvellous comment on Christ, the source of 'living water' from which we drink.[15] In praying, we also encounter the suffering of the People of God today. These prayers remind us of daily life and guide us in the encounter with today's people. They enlighten us in this encounter, because we do not only bring to it our own small intelligence, our love of God, but we learn through this Word of God also to bring God to them. They expect this of us: that we bring them the 'living water' of which St Columban speaks today. The people are thirsty and try to satisfy this thirst with various palliatives. But they understand well that these diversions are not the 'living water' that they need. The Lord is the source of 'living water'. But he says in chapter 7 of John that he who

---

15. The reading referred to is from Instruction 13 of St Columbanus from which is drawn the second reading of the Office of Readings for Thursday in the twenty-first week in Ordinary Time.

believes becomes a 'river' because he has drunk from Christ. And this 'living water' (cf. Jn 7: 38) becomes a fountain of water in us, a source for others. In this way we seek to drink it in prayer, in the celebration of Holy Mass, in reading: we seek to drink from this source so that it may become a source within us. And we can respond better to the thirst of people today if we have within us the 'living water', the divine reality, the reality of the Lord Jesus made flesh. Thus, we can respond better to the needs of our people.

This deals with the first question. What can we do? We always do all we can for the people – in the other questions, we will be able to return to this point – and we live with the Lord in order to respond to people's true thirst.

Your second question was: *Is there any hope for this Diocese, for this portion of the People of God that makes up this Diocese of Albano, and for the Church?* I respond without hesitation: yes! Of course we have hope: the Church is alive! We have 2,000 years of the Church's history with so much suffering and even so many failures: let us think of the Church in Asia Minor and the great and flourishing Church in North Africa which disappeared with the Muslim invasion. Thus, parts of the Church can truly disappear, as St John – or the Lord through John – said in the Book of Revelation: 'I will come to you and remove your lamp stand from its place, unless you repent' (2: 5). But, on the other hand, we perceive how the Church has re-emerged from so many crises with new youth, with a new freshness.

Actually, in the century of the Reformation, the Catholic Church seemed almost to have come to her end. This new current which declared: 'Now the Church of Rome is finished', seemed to triumph. And we see that with the great saints, such as Ignatius of Loyola, Teresa of Avila, Charles Borromeo and others, that the Church was resurrected. In the Council of Trent, she found a new actualization and the revitalization of her doctrine. And she lived again with great vitality. Let us look at the age of the Enlightenment, when Voltaire said: 'At last this ancient Church is dead, humanity is alive!' And instead, what happens? The Church is renewed.

The nineteenth century became the century of the great saints, of new vitality for a multitude of religious congregations, and faith is stronger than all the currents that come and go. And this also happened in the past century. Hitler once said: 'Providence called me, a Catholic, to have done with Catholicism. Only a Catholic can destroy Catholicism.' He was sure that he had all the means to be able at last to destroy Catholicism. Likewise, the great Marxist trend was convinced that it would achieve the scientific revision of the world and open doors to the future: the Church is nearing her end, she is done for! The Church, however, is stronger, as Christ said. It is Christ's life that wins through in his Church.

Even in difficult times when there is a shortage of vocations, the Word of the Lord lives for ever. And he who, as the Lord himself said, builds his life on this 'rock' of the Word of Christ, builds it well. Therefore, we can be confident. We also see new initiatives of faith in our day. We see that in Africa, despite all her problems, the Church has fresh new vocations, which is encouraging.

Thus, with all the differences of the historical prospect of today, we see – and not only see but believe – that the words of the Lord are spirit and life, they are words of eternal life. St Peter said, as we heard last Sunday in the Gospel: 'You have the words of eternal life; and we have believed, and have come to know that you are the Holy One of God' (Jn 6: 68-69). And in looking at the Church today, together with all the suffering we see the Church's vitality, and we ourselves can also say: we have believed and have come to know that you offer us the words of eternal life, hence, a never-failing hope.

Fr Vittorio Petruzzi, parochial vicar in Aprilia:

Your Holiness, for the pastoral year that is about to begin, our Diocese was asked by the Bishop to pay special attention to the Liturgy, in the theological dimension and in celebrative practices. The central theme for reflection at the residential weeks in which we shall be taking part in September is: 'The planning and implementation of the proclamation in the liturgical year, in sacraments and in sacramentals'. As priests, we are called to celebrate a 'serious, simple and beautiful liturgy', to use a beautiful formula contained in the document 'Communicating the Gospel in a Changing World' by the Italian Bishops. Holy Father, can you help us to understand how all this can be expressed in the 'ars celebrandi'?[16]

Pope Benedict XVI: *Ars celebrandi:* here too I would say that there are different dimensions. The first dimension is that the *celebratio* is prayer and a conversation with God: God with us and us with God. Thus, the first requirement for a good celebration is that the priest truly enter this colloquy. In proclaiming the Word, he feels himself in conversation with God. He is a listener to the Word and a preacher of the Word, in the sense that he makes himself an instrument of the Lord and seeks to understand this Word of God which he must then transmit to the people. He is in a conversation with God because the texts of Holy Mass are not theatrical scripts or anything like them, but prayers, thanks to which, together with the assembly, I speak to God.

It is important, therefore, to enter into this conversation. St Benedict in his 'Rule' tells the monks, speaking of the recitation of the Psalms, *'Mens concordet voci'*.[17] The *vox,* words, precede our mind. This is not usually the case: one has to think first, then

---

16. *The art/skill of celebrating* [the Liturgy].
17. This phrase is drawn from the writings of St Benedict and asks that our spirit should be in harmony with what our voices say.

one's thought becomes words. But here, the words come first. The sacred Liturgy gives us the words; we must enter into these words, find a harmony with this reality that precedes us.

In addition, we must also learn to understand the structure of the Liturgy and why it is laid out as it is. The Liturgy developed in the course of two millennia and even after the Reformation was not something worked out by simply a few liturgists. It has always remained a continuation of this on-going growth of worship and proclamation.

Thus, to be well in tune, it is very important to understand this structure that developed over time and to enter with our *mens* into the *vox* of the Church. To the extent that we have interiorized this structure, comprehended this structure, assimilated the words of the Liturgy, we can enter into this inner consonance and thus not only speak to God as individuals, but enter into the 'we' of the Church, which is praying. And we thus transform our 'I' in this way, by entering into the 'we' of the Church, enriching and enlarging this 'I', praying with the Church, with the words of the Church, truly being in conversation with God.

This is the first condition: we ourselves must interiorize the structure, the words of the Liturgy, the Word of God. Thus, our celebration truly becomes a celebration 'with' the Church: our hearts are enlarged and we are not doing just anything but are 'with' the Church, in conversation with God. It seems to me that people truly feel that we converse with God, with them, and that in this common prayer we attract others, in communion with the children of God we attract others; or if not, we are only doing something superficial.

Thus, the fundamental element of the true *ars celebrandi* is this consonance, this harmony between what we say with our lips and what we think with our heart. The '*Sursum corda*', which is a very ancient word of the Liturgy, should come before the Preface, before the Liturgy, as the 'path' for our speaking and thinking. We must raise our heart to the Lord, not only as a ritual response but as an expression of what is happening in this heart that is uplifted, and also lifts up others.

In other words, the *ars celebrandi* is not intended as an invitation to some sort of theatre or show, but to an interiority that makes itself felt and becomes acceptable and evident to the people taking part. Only if they see that this is not an exterior or spectacular *ars* – we are not actors! – but the expression of the journey of our heart that attracts their hearts too, will the Liturgy become beautiful, will it become the communion with the Lord of all who are present.

Of course, external things must also be associated with this fundamental condition, expressed in St Benedict's words: *'Mens concordet voci'* – the heart is truly raised, uplifted to the Lord. We must learn to say the words properly.

Sometimes, when I was still a teacher in my country, young people had read the Sacred Scriptures. And they read them as one reads the text of a poem one has not understood. Naturally, to learn to say words correctly one must first understand the text with its drama, with its immediacy. It is the same for the Preface and for the Eucharistic Prayer.

It is difficult for the faithful to follow a text as long as our Eucharistic Prayer. For this reason these new 'inventions' are constantly cropping up. However, with constantly new Eucharistic Prayers one does not solve the problem. The problem is that this is a moment that also invites others to silence with God and to pray with God. Therefore, things can only go better if the Eucharistic Prayer is said well and with the correct pauses for silence, if it is said with interiority but also with the art of speaking.

It follows that the recitation of the Eucharistic Prayer requires a moment of special attention if it is to be spoken in such a way that it involves others. I believe we should also find opportunities in catechesis, in homilies and in other circumstances to explain this Eucharistic Prayer well to the People of God so that they can follow the important moments – the account and the words of the Institution, the prayer for the living and the dead, the thanksgiving to the Lord and the *epiclesis* – if the community is truly to be involved in this prayer.

Thus, the words must be pronounced properly. There must then be an adequate preparation. Altar servers must know what to do; lectors must be truly experienced speakers. Then the choir, the singing, should be rehearsed: and let the altar be properly decorated. All this, even if it is a matter of many practical things, is part of the *ars celebrandi*.

But to conclude, the fundamental element is this art of entering into communion with the Lord, which we prepare for as priests throughout our lives.

APOSTOLIC JOURNEY OF HIS HOLINESS
BENEDICT XVI TO MUNICH, ALTÖTTING
AND REGENSBURG
(9–14 SEPTEMBER, 2006)

From the

ADDRESS TO A MEETING
OF THE PRIESTS AND
PERMANENT DEACONS OF
BAVARIA

Cathedral of St Mary and St Corbinian, Freising
Thursday, 14 September 2006

'Pilgrims and guides'

Now that I am back in this cathedral many memories come to
me as I see before me my old companions, and also the young
priests who are handing on the message, the torch of the faith.[18]
Memories of my ordination, of which Cardinal Wetter has spoken,
come to mind. Here I lay prostrate, enveloped by the litany of
all the saints, by the intercession of all the saints. I realized that
on this path we are not alone, that the great multitude of saints
walk with us, and the living saints, the faithful of today and

---

18. Pope Benedict XVI was ordained a priest with his brother in the
Cathedral at Freising. Later, as Archbishop of Munich and Freising, he
also ordained many young men there.

tomorrow, sustain us and walk with us. Then came the laying on of hands, and finally Cardinal Faulhaber proclaimed to us: '*Iam non dico vos servos sed amicos*' – 'I do not call you servants, but friends'; at that moment, I experienced my priestly ordination as an initiation into the community of Jesus' friends, called to be with him and to proclaim his message.

I am also reminded of the priests and deacons that I myself have ordained here. They are now dedicated to the service of the Gospel and for many years, decades even, they have been handing on the message, and they continue to do so. Naturally, I also recall the processions of Saint Corbinian. It was the custom then to open the reliquary. As the bishop's place was behind the urn, I had a direct view of the saint's skull. I saw myself taking part in the procession of centuries walking the way of the faith. In this great 'procession of time', I could see that we too can walk along, moving with it into the future. This became clear as the procession passed through the nearby cloister where so many children were gathered, and I would trace the sign of the cross on their foreheads. Today we are still living the same experience; we are in the great procession, in the pilgrimage of the Gospel. We can be both pilgrims and guides. By following those who have walked in the footsteps of Christ, we too are following him, and so we enter into the light.

Let us now come to the homily, in which I wish to make just two points. The first relates to the Gospel we have just heard, a passage which we all have heard so often, which we have interpreted and meditated in our hearts. 'The harvest is plentiful' says the Lord. In saying that it is 'plentiful', he is not simply referring to that particular moment and to those pathways of Palestine on which he journeyed during his earthly life: his words are valid for today. They mean that in people's hearts a harvest is growing; they mean, to put it another way, that deep within, people are waiting for God, waiting for a directive full of light to show the way forward, waiting for a message that is more than just words, hoping, waiting for that love which, beyond the present instant, will welcome and sustain us for eternity. The harvest is plentiful, and labourers are needed in every generation. The other part of the quotation: 'the labourers are few', is also true, if in a different sense, for every generation.

'Pray the Lord of the harvest to send out labourers'. This means that the harvest is ready, but God wishes to enlist helpers to bring it into the storehouse. God needs them. He needs people to say: yes, I am ready to become your harvest labourer; I am ready to offer help so that this harvest which is ripening in people's hearts may truly be brought into the storehouses of eternity and become an enduring, divine communion of joy and love. 'Pray the Lord of the harvest' also means that we cannot simply 'produce' vocations; they must come from God. This is not like other professions, we cannot simply recruit people by using the right kind of publicity or the correct type of strategy. The call which comes from the heart of God must always finds its way into the heart of man. And yet, precisely so that it may reach into hearts, our cooperation is needed. To pray the Lord of the harvest means above all to ask him for this, to stir his heart and say: 'Please do this! Rouse labourers! Enkindle in them enthusiasm and joy for the Gospel! Make them understand that this is a treasure greater than any other, and that whoever has discovered it, must hand it on!'

We stir the heart of God. But our prayer to God does not consist of words alone; the words must lead to action so that from our praying heart a spark of our joy in God and in the Gospel may arise, enkindling in the hearts of others a readiness to say 'yes'. As people of prayer, filled with his light, we reach out to others and bring them into our prayer and into the presence of God, who will not fail to do his part. In this sense we must continue to pray to the Lord of the harvest, to stir his heart, and together with God touch the hearts of others through our prayer. And he, according to his purpose, will bring to maturity their 'yes', their readiness to respond; the constancy, in other words, through all this world's perplexity, through the heat of the day and the darkness of the night, to persevere faithfully in his service. Hence they will know that their efforts, however arduous, are noble and worthwhile because they lead to what is essential, they ensure that people receive what they hope for: God's light and God's love.

The second point I wish to make is a practical matter. The number of priests has declined even if at the present moment we are able to cope, because we have young priests and old priests, and there are young men on their way towards the priesthood. And yet the burdens have increased. To be looking after two, three, or four parishes at the same time, in addition to all the new tasks that have emerged, can lead to discouragement. Often I ask myself, or rather each of us asks himself and his brethren: how are we going to cope? Is this not a profession that consumes us, that no longer brings us joy since we see that whatever we do is never enough? We are overburdened!

What response can be given? Obviously I cannot offer infallible remedies: nevertheless I wish to suggest some basic guidelines. I take the first one from the Letter to the Philippians (cf. 2: 5-8), where Saint Paul says to all, especially of course to those who work in God's field: 'have in yourselves the mind of Christ Jesus'. His mind was such that, faced with the destiny of humanity, he could hardly bear to remain in glory, but had to stoop down and do the incredible, take upon himself the utter poverty of a human life even to the point of suffering on the Cross. This is the mind of Jesus Christ: feeling impelled to bring to humanity the light of the Father, to help us by forming the Kingdom of God with us and in us. And the mind of Jesus Christ also deeply roots him in all-pervading communion with the Father.

An external indication of this, as it were, is that the Evangelists repeatedly recount that he withdraws to the mountain alone, to pray. His activity flows from his profound union with the Father, and precisely because of this, he has to go out and visit all the towns and villages proclaiming the Kingdom of God, announcing that it is present in our midst. He has to inaugurate the Kingdom among us so that, through us, it can transform the world; he has to ensure that God's will is done on earth as it is in Heaven and that Heaven comes down upon earth. These two aspects belong to the mind of Christ Jesus. On the one hand we must know God from within, know Christ from within, and be with him; only in this way will we discover the 'treasure'. On the other hand we must also go out towards others. We cannot simply keep the 'treasure' to ourselves; we must hand it on.

I would like to be more specific with regard to this basic guideline with its two aspects. It is necessary to combine zeal with humility, with an awareness of our limitations. On the one hand there has to be zeal: if we truly encounter Christ again and again, we cannot keep him to ourselves. We feel impelled to go out to the poor, the elderly, the weak, to children and young people, to those in their prime. We feel impelled to be 'heralds', apostles of Christ. Yet our zeal, lest it become empty and begin to wear us down, must be combined with humility, with moderation, with the acceptance of our limits. So many things should be done, yet I see that I am not capable of doing them. This is true, I imagine, for many pastors, and it is also true for the Pope, who ought to do so many things! My strength is simply not enough. In this way I learn to do what I can and I leave the rest to God and to my assistants, saying: 'Ultimately you must do this work, Lord, because the Church is yours. You give me only the energy I have. I give it to you, since it comes from you; everything else I place in your hands.' I believe that the humility which prompts us to say: 'my energy goes no further, I leave you, Lord, to do the rest' is crucial. And then trust is needed: he will give me the assistants I need, and they will do what I am unable to do.

To take this idea a step further, the combination of zeal and humility also means combining all aspects of service with our inner life. We can serve others and give to others only if we personally also receive, if we do not empty ourselves. That is why the Church offers us free spaces, which on the one hand allow us to 'breathe in' and 'breathe out' anew, and on the other hand become the source and centre of our service. In the first place there is the daily celebration of Holy Mass. We must never do this merely out of routine, as 'something that I have to do', but rather 'from within'! Let us identify with the words and actions, and with the event that is really present there! If we celebrate Mass prayerfully, if our saying 'this is my body' is born from our communion with Jesus Christ who has laid his hands upon us and authorized us to speak with his own 'I', if we celebrate the Eucharist with intimate participation in faith and prayer, then it is not simply an external duty; then the *ars celebrandi* comes naturally, because it consists in celebrating from the Lord's perspective and in communion with him, and hence in the way that best serves the people. Then we ourselves are constantly enriched and at the same time, we hand on to others something more than what is ours, that is to say: the Lord's presence.

The other free space to which the Church, so to speak, obliges us, and in so doing liberates us, is the Liturgy of the Hours. Let us aim to recite it as a true prayer, a prayer in communion with the Israel of the Old and New Testaments, a prayer in communion with all who pray throughout history, a prayer in communion with Jesus Christ, a prayer that arises from the deepest 'I', from the deepest subject of these prayers. In this way we draw into our prayer those others who lack the time or the energy or the capacity to pray. As people of prayer, we represent others when we pray and in so doing, we fulfil a pastoral ministry of the first order. This is not withdrawing into the private sphere, it is a pastoral priority, it is a pastoral activity in which our own priesthood is renewed, and we are once again filled by Christ. We include others in the communion of the praying Church and at the same time, we allow the power of prayer, the presence of Jesus Christ, to flow into this world.

The motto of these days has been: 'those who believe are never alone'.[19] These words apply and must apply especially to priests, to each one of us. They apply in two senses: a priest is never alone because Jesus Christ is always with him. He is with us, let us also be with him! But they must apply in another sense too. He who becomes a priest enters into a presbyterate, a community of priests together with their Bishop. He is a priest in this communion with his confrères. Let us commit ourselves to live this out, not only as a theological and juridical precept, but as a practical experience for each of us. Let us offer this communion to one another, let us offer it especially to those that we know are suffering from loneliness, those that we know are troubled by questions and problems, and perhaps by doubts and uncertainties! Let us offer this communion to each other, and so experience our communion with Jesus Christ ever anew, more fully and more joyfully, through being with the other, through being with others! Amen.

19. The motto of this particular Papal Pastoral Visit.

From an

ADDRESS TO THE CONFESSORS WHO SERVE IN THE FOUR PAPAL BASILICAS OF ROME

Clementine Hall
Monday, 19 February 2007

'Minister of the consoling mercy of God'

The Sacrament of Penance, which has such importance in the Christian life, renders present the redemptive efficacy of Christ's Paschal Mystery. In imparting absolution, pronounced in the name and on behalf of the Church, the confessor becomes the conscious means of a wonderful event of grace.

With docile compliance to the Magisterium of the Church, he makes himself minister of the consoling mercy of God, he draws attention to the reality of sin, and at the same time he manifests the boundless renewing power of divine love, love that gives back life.

Therefore, confession becomes a spiritual rebirth that transforms the penitent into a new creature. Only God's grace can work this miracle, and it is accomplished through the words and gestures of the priest.

By experiencing the tenderness and pardon of the Lord, the penitent is more easily led to acknowledge the gravity of sin, is more resolved to avoid it in order to remain and grow in renewed friendship with him.

In this mysterious process of interior renewal the confessor is not a passive spectator, but *persona dramatis,* that is, an active instrument of divine mercy. Therefore, it is necessary that to a good spiritual and pastoral sensibility he unites a serious theological, moral and pedagogical preparation that enables him to understand the life of the person.

Furthermore, it is very useful for him to know the social, cultural and professional environment of those who approach the confessional in order to be able to offer appropriate advice and spiritual practices and orientations.

May the priest not forget that in this Sacrament he is called to take on the role of father, spiritual guide, teacher and educator. This demands constant updating: this is also the aim of the so-called 'internal forum' promoted by the Apostolic Penitentiary.

Dear priests, your ministry bears above all a spiritual character. To human wisdom, to theological preparation, therefore, one must add a profound spiritual disposition, nourished by prayerful contact with Christ, Master and Redeemer.

In virtue of presbyteral ordination, in fact, the confessor carries out a particular service *'in persona Christi',* with a fullness of human gifts that are strengthened by grace.

His model is Jesus, the One sent by the Father: the source from which to draw abundantly is the vivifying breath of the Holy Spirit. Before such a lofty responsibility human strength is surely inadequate, but the humble and faithful adherence to the salvific design of Christ renders us, dear brothers, witnesses of the universal Redemption worked by him, putting into effect the admonition of St Paul who says: 'God was in Christ reconciling the world to himself . . . and entrusting to us the message of reconciliation' (II Cor 5: 19).

To fulfil such a duty we must, above all, root this message of salvation in ourselves and let it transform us deeply. We cannot preach pardon and reconciliation to others if we are not personally penetrated by it. As it is true that in our ministry there are various ways and instruments to communicate the merciful love of God to our brethren, it is, however, in the celebration of this Sacrament that we can do it in the most complete and eminent way.

Christ has chosen us, dear priests, to be the only ones to be able to pardon sins in his Name: it concerns, then, a specific ecclesial service to which we must give priority.

How many people in difficulty seek the comfort and consolation of Christ! How many penitents find in confession the peace and joy that they sought for so long! How can one not recognize also in our age, marked by so many religious and social challenges, that this Sacrament also be rediscovered and proposed anew?

Dear brothers, let us follow the example of the saints, in particular those who, like you, were almost exclusively dedicated to the ministry of the confessional. Among them are St Jean-Marie Vianney, St Leopold Mandic, and closer to us, St Pio of Pietrelcina.

May they help you from heaven to be able to abundantly dispense the mercy and pardon of Christ. May Mary, Refuge of Sinners, obtain for you the strength, encouragement and hope to generously continue your indispensable mission.

I assure you of my heartfelt prayer, while with affection I bless you all.

From the

ADDRESS GIVEN AT THE LENTEN MEETING WITH THE CLERGY OF ROME

Hall of Blessings
Thursday, 22 February 2007

A little while ago I read what St Augustine said in Book X of his *Confessions*: 'I was tempted and I now understand that it was a temptation to enclose myself in contemplative life, to seek solitude with you, O Lord; but you prevented me, you plucked me from it and made me listen to St Paul's words: "Christ died for us all. Consequently, we must die with Christ and live for all." I understood that I cannot shut myself up in contemplation; you died for us all. Therefore, with you, I must live for all and thus practise works of charity. True contemplation is expressed in works of charity. Therefore, the sign for which we have truly prayed, that we have experienced in the encounter with Christ, is that we exist "for others".'

This is what a parish priest must be like. And St Augustine was a great parish priest. He said: 'In my life I also always longed to spend my life listening to the Word in meditation, but now – day after day, hour after hour – I must stand at the door where the bell is always ringing, I must comfort the afflicted, help the poor, reprimand those who are quarrelsome, create peace and so forth.'

St Augustine lists all the tasks of a parish priest, for at that time the bishop was also what the *Kadi* in Islamic countries is today. With regard to problems of civil law, let us say, he was the judge of peace: he had to encourage peace between the litigants. He therefore lived a life that for him, a contemplative, was very difficult. But he understood this truth: thus, I am with Christ; in existing 'for others', I am in the Crucified and Risen Lord.

I think this is a great consolation for parish priests and bishops. Even if little time is left for contemplation, in being 'for others', we are with the Lord.

Fr Angelo Mangano, Parish Priest of San Gelasio. He pointed out the importance of developing unity between spiritual life and pastoral life, which is not an organizational technique but integral to the life of the Church itself. Fr Mangano asked the Holy Father how to spread the concept of pastoral service among God's People as the true life of the Church, and how to ensure that pastoral work is always nourished by conciliar ecclesiology.

Pope Benedict XVI: I think there are several questions here. One question is: how can we inspire parishes with conciliar ecclesiology and make the faithful live this ecclesiology? Another is how should we behave and make pastoral work spiritual within us?

Let us start with the latter question. There is always a certain tension between what I absolutely have to do and what spiritual reserves I must have. I always see it in St Augustine, who complains about this in his preaching. I have already cited him: 'I long to live with the Word of God from morning to night but I have to be with you.' Augustine nonetheless finds this balance by being always available but also by keeping for himself moments of prayer and meditation on the Sacred Word, because otherwise he would no longer be able to say anything.

Here in particular, I would like to underline what you said

about the fact that pastoral work must never be mere strategy or administrative work but must always be a spiritual task. Nor, of course, can the latter be totally lacking either, because we are on this earth and such problems exist: the efficient management of money, etc. This too is a sector that cannot be totally ignored.

Nonetheless, the fundamental emphasis must be on the very fact that being a pastor is in itself a spiritual act. You rightly referred to John's Gospel, chapter 10, in which the Lord describes himself as the 'Good Shepherd'. And as a first definitive moment, Jesus says that the pastor goes first. In other words, it is he who shows the way, he is the first to be an example to others, the first to take the road that is the road for others. The pastor leads the way.

This means that he himself lives first of all on the Word of God; he is a man of prayer, a man of forgiveness, a man who receives and celebrates the sacraments as acts of prayer and encounter with the Lord. He is a man of charity, lived and practised, thus all the simple acts, conversation, encounter, everything that needs to be done, become spiritual acts in communion with Christ. His *'pro omnibus'* becomes our *'pro meis'*.[20]

Then, he goes before us and I think that in having mentioned this 'leading the way', the essential has already been said. Chapter 10 of John continues, saying that Jesus goes before us, giving himself on the Cross. And this is also inevitable for the priest. The offering of himself is also participation in the Cross of Christ, and thanks to this we too can credibly comfort the suffering and be close to the poor, the marginalized, etc.

Therefore, in this programme that you have developed, it is

---

20. His *for all* [people] becomes our *for my people* [i.e. my friends and relations etc.].

fundamental to spiritualize daily pastoral work. It is easier to say this than to do it, but we must try.

Moreover, to be able to spiritualize our work, we must again follow the Lord. The Gospels tell us that by day he worked and by night he was on the mountain with his Father, praying. Here, I must confess my weakness. At night I cannot pray, at night I want to sleep. However, a little free time for the Lord is really necessary: either the celebration of Mass or the prayer of the Liturgy of the Hours and even a brief daily meditation following the Liturgy, the Rosary. But this personal conversation with the Word of God is important; it is only in this way that we can find the reserves to respond to the demands of pastoral life.

The second point: you rightly underlined the ecclesiology of the Council. It seems to me that we must interiorize this ecclesiology far more, that of *Lumen Gentium* and of *Ad Gentes,* which is also an ecclesiological Document, as well as the ecclesiology of the minor Documents and of *Dei Verbum.*

By interiorizing this vision we can also attract our people to this vision, which understands that the Church is not merely a large structure, one of these supranational bodies that exist. Although she is a body, the Church is the Body of Christ, hence, she is a spiritual body, as St Paul said. She is a spiritual reality. I think this is very important: that people see that the Church is not a supranational organization nor an administrative body or power, that she is not a social agency, but indeed that although she does social and supranational work, she is a spiritual body.

I consider that in our prayers with the people, listening with the people to the Word of God, celebrating the sacraments with the People of God, acting with Christ in charity, etc., and especially in our homilies, we should disseminate this vision. It seems to me, in this regard, that the homily affords a marvellous opportunity to be close to the people and to communicate the spirituality taught by the Council. And it thus seems to me that if the homily is developed from prayer, from listening to the Word of God, it is a communication of the content of the Word of God.

The Council truly reaches out to our people, not those fragments in the press that presented an erroneous image of the Council but the true spirituality of the Council. Thus, we must always learn the Word of God anew, with the Council and in the spirit of the Council, interiorizing its vision. By so doing, we can also communicate with our people and thus truly carry out a task that is both pastoral and spiritual.

From an

ADDRESS TO THE PARTICIPANTS IN THE COURSE ON THE INTERNAL FORUM PROMOTED BY THE APOSTOLIC PENITENTIARY

Clementine Hall
Friday, 16 March 2007

Instruments of the merciful love of God

Today's meeting also offers me the opportunity to reflect together with you on the importance in our day of the Sacrament of Penance and to repeat the necessity for priests to prepare themselves to administer it with devotion and fidelity to the praise of God and for the sanctification of the Christian people, as they promise to their bishop on the day of their priestly ordination.

In fact, it is one of the qualifying duties of the special ministry that they are called to exercise *'in persona Christi'*. With the gestures and sacramental words the priest above all makes God's love visible, which was revealed fully in Christ.

In the administration of the Sacrament of Pardon and of Reconciliation, the priest – as the Catechism of the Catholic Church recalls – acts as 'the sign and the instrument of God's merciful love for the sinner' (n. 1465). What takes place in this Sacrament, therefore, is especially a mystery of love, a work of the merciful love of the Lord.

'God is love' (I Jn 4: 16): in this simple affirmation the Evangelist John has enclosed the revelation of the entire mystery of the Triune God. And in meeting with Nicodemus, Jesus, foretelling his passion and death on the Cross, affirms: 'For God so loved the world that he gave his only Son, that whoever believes in him should not perish but have eternal life' (Jn 3: 16).

We all need to draw from the inexhaustible fountain of divine love, which is totally manifested to us in the mystery of the Cross, in order to find authentic peace with God, with ourselves and with our neighbour. Only from this spiritual source is it possible to draw the indispensable interior energy to overcome the evil and sin in the ceaseless battle that marks our earthly pilgrimage toward the heavenly homeland.

The contemporary world continues to present contradictions so clearly outlined by the Fathers of the Second Vatican Council (cf. *Gaudium et Spes*, nn. 4-10): we see a humanity that would like to be self-sufficient, where more than a few consider it almost possible to do without God in order to live well; and yet how many seem sadly condemned to face the dramatic situations of an empty existence, how much violence there still is on the earth, how much solitude weighs on the soul of the humanity of the communications era!

In a word, it seems that today there is even loss of the 'sense of sin', but in compensation the 'guilt complex' has increased.

Who can free the heart of humankind from this yoke of death if not the One who by dying overcame for ever the power of evil with the omnipotence of divine love?

As St Paul reminded the Christians of Ephesus: 'God, who is rich in mercy, out of the great love with which he loved us, even when we were dead through our trespasses, made us alive together with Christ' (Eph 2: 4).

The priest in the Sacrament of Confession is the instrument

of this merciful love of God, whom he invokes in the formula of the absolution of sins: 'God, the Father of mercies, through the death and Resurrection of his Son, has reconciled the world to himself and sent the Holy Spirit among us for the forgiveness of sins; through the ministry of the Church, may God grant you pardon and peace.'

The New Testament speaks on every page of God's love and mercy, which are made visible in Christ. Jesus, in fact, who 'receives sinners and eats with them' (Lk 15: 2), and with authority affirms: 'Man, your sins are forgiven you' (Lk 5: 20), says: 'Those who are well have no need of a physician, but those who are sick do; I have not come to call the righteous, but sinners to repentance' (Lk 5: 31-32).

The duty of the priest and the confessor is primarily this: to bring every person to experience the love of Christ, encountering him on the path of their own lives as Paul met him on the road to Damascus. We know the impassioned declaration of the Apostle to the Gentiles after that meeting which changed his life: '[he] loved me and gave himself for me' (Gal 2: 20).

This is his personal experience on the way to Damascus: the Lord Jesus loved Paul and gave himself for him. And in Confession this is also our way, our way to Damascus, our experience: Jesus has loved me and has given himself for me.

May every person have this same spiritual experience and, as the Servant of God John Paul II said, rediscover 'Christ as *mysterium pietatis*,[21] the one in whom God shows us his compassionate heart and reconciles us fully with himself. It is this face of Christ that must be rediscovered through the Sacrament of Penance' (John Paul II, *Novo Millennio Ineunte*, n. 37).

The priest, minister of the Sacrament of Reconciliation, must always consider it his duty to make transpire, in words and in

---

21. *The mystery of piety [religion].*

drawing near to the penitent, the merciful love of God. Like the father in the parable of the prodigal son, to welcome the penitent sinner, to help him rise again from sin, to encourage him to amend himself, never making pacts with evil but always taking up again the way of evangelical perfection. May this beautiful experience of the prodigal son, who finds the fullness of divine mercy in the father, be the experience of whoever confesses in the Sacrament of Reconciliation.

Dear brothers, all this means that the priest engaged in the ministry of the Sacrament of Penance is himself motivated by a constant tending to holiness. The Catechism of the Catholic Church aims high in this demand when it affirms: 'The confessor . . . should have a proven knowledge of Christian behaviour, experience of human affairs, respect and sensitivity toward the one who has fallen; he must love the truth, be faithful to the Magisterium of the Church, and lead the penitent with patience toward healing and full maturity. He must pray and do penance for his penitent, entrusting him to the Lord's mercy' (n. 1466).

To be able to fulfil this important mission, always interiorly united to the Lord, the priest must be faithful to the Church's Magisterium concerning moral doctrine, aware that the law of good and evil is not determined by the situation, but by God.

I ask the Virgin Mary, Mother of Mercy, to sustain the ministry of priest confessors and to help every Christian community to understand ever more the value and importance of the Sacrament of Penance for the spiritual growth of every one of the faithful. To you present here and to the people dear to you, I impart my Blessing with affection.

APOSTOLIC JOURNEY OF HIS HOLINESS
BENEDICT XVI TO BRAZIL ON THE
OCCASION OF THE FIFTH GENERAL
CONFERENCE OF THE BISHOPS OF
LATIN AMERICA AND THE CARIBBEAN

From the

ADDRESS GIVEN AFTER THE RECITATION OF THE HOLY ROSARY WITH PRIESTS, MEN RELIGIOUS, WOMEN RELIGIOUS, SEMINARIANS AND DEACONS

Basilica of the Shrine of Aparecida
Saturday, 12 May 2007

'The Church is our home!'

Just as the Apostles, together with Mary, 'went up to the upper room' and there, 'with one accord devoted themselves to prayer' (Acts 1: 13-14), so too we are gathered here today at the Shrine of Our Lady of Aparecida, which at this time is our 'upper room' where Mary, Mother of the Lord, is in our midst. Today it is she who leads our meditation; it is she who teaches us to pray. It is she who shows us the way to open our minds and hearts to the power of the Holy Spirit, who comes to fill the whole world.

We have just prayed the rosary. Through these sequences of meditations, the divine Comforter seeks to initiate us in the knowledge of Christ that issues forth from the clear source of the Gospel text. For her part, the Church of the third millennium proposes to offer Christians the capacity for 'knowledge – according to the words of Saint Paul – of God's mystery, of Christ, in whom are hid all the treasures of wisdom and knowledge' (Col 2: 2-3). Mary Most Holy, the pure and immaculate Virgin, is for us a school of faith destined to guide us and give us strength on the path that leads us to the Creator of Heaven and Earth. The Pope has come to Aparecida with great joy so as to say to you first of all: 'Remain in the school of Mary.' Take inspiration from her teachings, seek to welcome and to preserve in your hearts the enlightenment that she, by divine mandate, sends you from on high.

How beautiful it is to be gathered here in the name of Christ, in faith, in fraternity, in joy, in peace and in prayer, together with 'Mary, the mother of Jesus' (Acts 1: 14). How beautiful it is, my dear Priests, Deacons, Consecrated men and women, Seminarians and Christian families, to be here in the National Shrine of Our Lady of Aparecida, which is God's Dwelling-place, the House of Mary and the House of the Brothers; and in the coming days it is also to serve as the setting for the Fifth General Conference of the Bishops of Latin America and the Caribbean. How beautiful it is to be here in this Marian Basilica, towards which, at this time, the gaze and the hopes of the Christian world are turned, especially for the Christians of Latin America and the Caribbean!

I greet the dear priests who are present, and I keep in my thoughts and prayers all the priests spread throughout the world, especially those in Latin America and the Caribbean, including the *fidei donum* priests. What great challenges, what difficult situations you have to face, with such generosity, self-denial, sacrifices and renunciations! Your faithfulness in the exercise of the ministry and the life of prayer, your search for holiness, your total self-giving to God at the service of your brothers and sisters, as you expend your lives and energy in order to promote justice, fraternity, solidarity and sharing – all this speaks powerfully to my pastoral heart. The witness of a priestly life well lived brings nobility to the Church, calls forth admiration among the faithful, and is a source of blessings for the community; it is the best way to promote vocations, the most authentic invitation to other young people to respond positively to the Lord's call. It is true collaboration in building the Kingdom of God!

I thank you sincerely and I encourage you to continue living in a manner worthy of the vocation you have received. May the missionary fervour, the passion for an increasingly contemporary approach to evangelization, the authentic apostolic spirit and the zeal for souls always be present in your lives! My affection, my prayers and my thanks go also to the elderly and infirm priests. Your conformation to Christ Suffering and Risen is the most fruitful apostolate. Many thanks!

Dear Deacons and Seminarians, you have a special place in the Pope's heart, and so I extend to you too my most fraternal and heartfelt greetings. Your exuberance, enthusiasm, idealism and encouragement to face new challenges boldly serve to give the People of God a renewed openness, make the faithful more dynamic and help the community to grow, to progress, and to become more trusting, joyful and optimistic. I thank you for the witness that you bear, working together with your bishops in the pastoral activities of your dioceses. Always keep before your eyes the figure of Jesus, the Good Shepherd, who 'came not to be served but to serve, and to give his life as a ransom for many' (Mt 20: 28). Be like the first deacons of the Church: men of good reputation, filled with the Holy Spirit, with wisdom and with faith (cf. Acts 6: 3-5). And you, seminarians, give thanks to God for the call that he addresses to you. Remember that the seminary is the cradle of your vocation and the first place where you experience communal life (cf. *Directory for the Ministry and Life of Priests*, 32). I ask you, with God's help, to be holy faithful and happy priests in the service of the Church!

APOSTOLIC JOURNEY OF HIS HOLINESS BENEDICT XVI TO BRAZIL ON THE OCCASION OF THE FIFTH GENERAL CONFERENCE OF THE BISHOPS OF LATIN AMERICA AND THE CARIBBEAN

From the

ADDRESS GIVEN AT THE INAUGURAL SESSION OF THE FIFTH GENERAL CONFERENCE OF THE BISHOPS OF LATIN AMERICA AND THE CARIBBEAN

Conference Hall, Shrine of Aparecida
Sunday, 13 May 2007

'A man of God'

The first promoters of discipleship and mission are those who have been called 'to be with Jesus and to be sent out to preach' (cf. Mk 3: 14), that is, *the priests*. They must receive preferential attention and paternal care from their bishops, because they are the primary instigators of authentic renewal of Christian life among the People of God. I should like to offer them a word of paternal affection, hoping that 'the Lord will be their portion and cup' (cf. Ps 16: 5). If the priest has God as the foundation and centre of his life, he will experience the joy and the fruitfulness of his vocation. The priest must be above all a 'man of God' (I Tim 6: 11) who knows God directly, who has a profound personal friendship with Jesus, who shares with others the same sentiments that Christ has (cf. Phil 2: 5). Only in this way will the priest be capable of leading men to God, incarnate in Jesus Christ, and of being the representative of his love. In order to accomplish his lofty task, the priest must have a solid spiritual formation, and the whole of his life must be imbued with faith, hope and charity. Like Jesus, he must be one who seeks, through prayer, the face and the will of God, and he must be attentive to his cultural and intellectual preparation.

Dear priests of this Continent, and those of you who have come here to work as missionaries, the Pope accompanies you in your pastoral work and wants you to be full of joy and hope; above all he prays for you.

From the

ADDRESS TO THE BISHOPS OF THE EPISCOPAL CONFERENCE OF MALI ON THEIR 'AD LIMINA' VISIT

Papal Residence, Castel Gandolfo
Friday, 18 May 2007

In prayer and in activity, united to the Lord

Guided by sincere charity and special concern, you are a father, brother and friend to each of your priests. They cooperate generously in your apostolic mission, and often while living in humanly and spiritually difficult situations.

While the diocesan clergy today are called to play a more active role in evangelization, in fraternal and trusting collaboration with the missionaries – whose courageous work I acknowledge – priests must live their priestly identity by giving themselves to the Lord for the impartial service of their brethren without losing heart in the face of the difficulties they have to confront.

In ever more intimate communion with the One who called them, they will find unity in their life and, despite their diverse daily occupations, strength for their ministry at the service of the men and women entrusted to their care.

Prayer life and sacramental life are an authentic pastoral priority for priests, which will help them to respond with determination to the call to holiness they have received from the Lord, and to their mission to lead the faithful on the same path. May they never forget, as I wrote in my Encyclical *Deus Caritas Est*: 'People who pray are not wasting their time, even though the situation appears desperate and seems to call for action alone' (n. 36).

If priests are to be effective in their work of evangelization and contribute to the spiritual growth of the Christian community, their formation must be planned with great care. Formation, in fact, is not limited to passing on abstract notions. It must train candidates for the priestly ministry while being effectively linked to the realities of mission and of the presbyteral life.

Human formation is the basis of priestly formation. Special attention to the candidates' emotional maturity will enable them to give a free response to life in celibacy and chastity, a precious gift from God. It will also enable them to have a soundly established awareness of this throughout their lives.

From the

ADDRESS TO THE BISHOPS FROM THE DOMINICAN REPUBLIC ON THEIR 'AD LIMINA' VISIT

Thursday, 5 July 2007

The family of the priesthood

Taking into account that 'the presbyterate thus appears as a true family' (*Pastores Dabo Vobis,* n. 74), it is desirable that the bonds of charity between the bishop and his priests be very strong and cordial. If young men see that priests live a true spirituality of communion around their bishop, witnessing to union and charity among themselves, to Gospel charity and missionary availability, they themselves will feel more attracted to the priestly vocation.

It is of paramount importance that bishops pay special attention to their principal collaborators, the priests (cf. *Presbyterorum Ordinis,* n. 8), that they be impartial in their dealings with them, closely acquainted with their personal and pastoral needs, fatherly to them in their difficulties and that they give constant encouragement to their priests' work and endeavours and, in the context of the new evangelization, that they reach out to those who have distanced themselves.

From the

MEETING WITH THE CLERGY OF THE DIOCESES OF BELLUNO-FELTRE AND TREVISO

Church of St Justin Martyr, Auronzo di Cadore
Tuesday, 24 July 2007

Pope Benedict was asked by Fr Mauro, a priest present at this meeting, 'in exercising our pastoral ministry we are increasingly burdened by many duties. Our tasks in the management and administration of parishes, pastoral organization and assistance to people in difficulty are piling up. I ask you, what are the priorities we should aim for in our ministry as priests and parish priests?'

Pope Benedict XVI: That is a very realistic question, is it not? I am also somewhat familiar with this problem, with all the daily procedures, with all the necessary audiences, with all that there is to do. Yet, it is necessary to determine the right priorities and not to forget the essential: the proclamation of the Kingdom of God.

On hearing your question, I remembered the Gospel of two weeks ago on the mission of the seventy disciples. For this first important mission which Jesus had them undertake, the Lord gave them three orders which on the whole I think express the great priorities in the work of a disciple of Christ, a priest, in our day too. The three imperatives are: to pray, to provide care, to preach. I think we should find the balance between these three basic imperatives and keep them ever present as the heart of our work.

Prayer: which is to say, without a personal relationship with God nothing else can function, for we cannot truly bring God, the divine reality or true human life to people unless we ourselves live them in a deep, true relationship of friendship with God in Jesus Christ. Hence, the daily celebration of the Holy Eucharist is a fundamental encounter where the Lord speaks to me and I speak to the Lord who gives himself through my hands. Without the prayer of the Hours, in which we join in the great prayer of the entire People of God beginning with the Psalms of the ancient people who are renewed in the faith of the Church, and without personal prayer, we cannot be good priests for we would lose the essence of our ministry. The first imperative is to be a man of God, in the sense of a man in friendship with Christ and with his Saints.

Then comes the second command. Jesus said: tend the sick, seek those who have strayed, those who are in need. This is the Church's love for the marginalized and the suffering. Rich people can also be inwardly marginalized and suffering. 'To take care of' refers to all human needs, which are always profoundly oriented to God. Thus, as has been said, it is necessary for us to know our sheep, to be on good terms with the people entrusted to us, to have human contact and not to lose our humanity, because God was made man and consequently strengthened all dimensions of our being as humans. However, as I said, the human and the divine always go hand in hand. To my mind, the sacramental ministry is also part of this 'tending' in its multiple forms. The ministry of Reconciliation is an act of extraordinary caring which the person needs in order to be perfectly healthy. Thus, this sacramental care begins with Baptism, which is the fundamental renewal of our life, and extends to the Sacrament of Reconciliation and the Anointing of the Sick. Of course, all the other sacraments and also the Eucharist involve great care for souls. We have to care for people but above all – this is our mandate – for their souls. We must think of the many illnesses and moral and spiritual needs that exist today and that we must face, guiding people to the encounter with Christ in the sacrament, helping them to discover prayer and meditation, being silently recollected in church with this presence of God.

And then, preaching. What do we preach? We proclaim the Kingdom of God. But the Kingdom of God is not a distant utopia in a better world which may be achieved in 50 years' time, or who knows when. The Kingdom of God is God himself, God close to us who became very close in Christ. This is the Kingdom of God: God himself is near to us and we must draw close to this God who is close for he was made man, remains man and is always with us in his Word, in the Most Holy Eucharist and in all believers. Therefore, proclaiming the Kingdom of God means speaking of God today, making present God's words, the Gospel which is God's presence and, of course, making present the God who made himself present in the Holy Eucharist.

By interweaving these three priorities and, naturally, taking into account all the human aspects, including our own limitations that we must recognize, we can properly fulfil our priesthood. This humility that recognizes the limitations of our own strength is important as well. All that we cannot do, the Lord must do. And there is also the ability to delegate and to collaborate. All this must always go with the fundamental imperatives of praying, tending and preaching.

Fr Saverio asked a question concerning the missions: 'This year is the 50th anniversary of the Encyclical Fidei Donum. *Many priests in our diocese, myself included, have accepted the Pope's invitation,*[22] *they, we, have lived and are living the experience of the mission*

---

22. The Pope being referred to is Pope Pius XII who published the Encyclical *Fidei Donum* (The Gift of Faith) on 21 April 1957.

ad gentes. *There can be no doubt that this is an extraordinary experience which in my modest opinion could be shared by a great number of priests with a view to exchanges between sister churches. Since the instruction in the encyclical is still timely today, given the dwindling number of priests in our countries, how and with what attitude should it be accepted and lived both by the priests who are sent out and by the whole diocese? Thank you.'*

Pope Benedict XVI: Thank you. I would first like to thank all these *fidei donum* priests and the dioceses. As I have already mentioned, I have received a great number of *ad limina* visits from bishops of Asia, Africa and Latin America and they all tell me: 'We are badly in need of *fidei donum* priests and we are deeply grateful for the work they do. They make present, often in extremely difficult situations, the catholicity of the Church and they make visible the great universal communion which we form, as well as the love for our distant neighbour who becomes close in the situation of the *fidei donum* priest.'

In the past 50 years I have almost tangibly felt and seen this great gift, truly given, in my conversations with priests who say to us: 'Do not think that we Africans are now quite self-sufficient; we are still in need of the visibility of the great communion of the universal Church.' I would say that we all need to be visible as Catholics and we need to love the neighbour who comes from afar and thus finds his neighbour.

Today, the situation has changed in the sense that we in Europe also receive priests from Africa, Latin America and even from other parts of Europe. This enables us to perceive the beauty of this exchange of gifts, this gift of one to the other, because we all need one another: it is precisely in this way that the Body of Christ grows. To sum up, I would like to say that this gift was and is a great gift, perceived in the Church as such: in so many situations that I cannot describe here, which involve social problems, problems of development, problems of the proclamation of the faith, problems of loneliness, the need for the presence of others, these priests are a gift in which the dioceses and particular Churches recognize the presence of Christ who gives himself for us. At the same time, they recognize that Eucharistic Communion is not only a supranatural communion but becomes concrete communion in this gift of self of diocesan priests who make themselves available to other dioceses, and that the network of particular Churches thus truly becomes a network of love. Thanks to all those who have made this gift.

I can only encourage bishops and priests to continue making this gift. I know that today, with the shortage of vocations, it is becoming more and more difficult in Europe to make this gift; but we already have the experience that other continents in turn, such as especially India and Africa, also give us priests. Reciprocity continues to be of paramount importance. Precisely the experience that we are the Church sent out into the world which everyone knows and loves, is very necessary and also constitutes the power of proclamation. Thus, people can see that the mustard seed bears fruit and ceaselessly, time and again, becomes a great tree in which the birds of the air find repose. Thank you and be strong.

I am Fr Francesco. Holy Father, one sentence you wrote in your book made a deep impression on me: '[But] what did Jesus actually bring if not world peace, universal prosperity and a better world? What has he brought? The answer is very simple: "God. He has brought God"' (Jesus of Nazareth, English edition, p. 44); I find the clarity and truth of this citation disarming. This is my question: there is talk about the new evangelization, the new proclamation of the Gospel – this was also the main theme of the Synod of our Diocese, Belluno-Feltre – but what should we do so that this God, the one treasure brought by Jesus and who all too often appears hazy to many, shines forth anew in our homes and becomes the water that quenches even the thirst of the many who seem no longer to be thirsting? Thank you.

Pope Benedict XVI: Thank you. Yours is a fundamental question. The fundamental question of our pastoral work is how to bring God to the world, to our contemporaries. Of course, bringing God is a multi-dimensional task: already in Jesus' preaching, in his life and his death we see how this One develops in so many dimensions.

I think that we should always be mindful of two things: on the one hand, the Christian proclamation. Christianity is not a highly complicated collection of so many dogmas that it is impossible for anyone to know them all; it is not something exclusively for academicians who can study these things, but it is something simple: God exists and God is close in Jesus Christ. Thus, to sum up, Jesus Christ himself said that the Kingdom of God had arrived. Basically, what we preach is one, simple thing. All the dimensions subsequently revealed are dimensions of this one thing and all people do not have to know everything but must certainly enter into the depths and into the essential. In this way, the different dimensions also unfold with ever increasing joy.

But in practice what should be done? I think, speaking of pastoral work today, that we have already touched on the essential points. But to continue in this direction, bringing God implies above all, on the one hand, love, and on the other, hope and faith. Thus, the dimension of life lived, bearing the best witness for Christ, the best proclamation, is always the life of true Christians. If we see that families nourished by faith live in joy, that they also experience suffering in profound and fundamental joy, that they help others, loving God and their neighbour, in my opinion this is the most beautiful proclamation today.

For me too, the most comforting proclamation is always that of seeing Catholic families or personalities who are penetrated by faith: the presence of God truly shines out in them and they bring the 'living water' that you mentioned. The fundamental proclamation is, therefore, precisely that of the actual life of Christians. Of course, there is also the proclamation of the Word. We must spare no effort to ensure that the Word is listened to and known. Today, there are numerous schools of the Word and of the conversation with God in Sacred Scripture, a conversation which necessarily also becomes prayer, because the purely theoretical study of Sacred Scripture is a form of listening that is merely intellectual and would not be a real or satisfactory encounter with the Word of God. If it is true that in Scripture and in the Word of God it is the Living Lord God who speaks to us, who elicits our response and our prayers, then schools of Scripture must also be schools of prayer, of dialogue with God, of drawing intimately close to God: consequently, the whole proclamation. Then, of course, I would say the sacraments.

All the saints also always come with God. It is important – Sacred Scripture tells us from the very outset – that God never comes by himself but comes accompanied and surrounded by the angels and saints. In the great stained glass window in St Peter's which portrays the Holy Spirit, what I like so much is the fact that God is surrounded by a throng of angels and living beings who are an expression, an emanation, so to speak, of God's love.

And with God, with Christ, with the man who is God and with God who is man, Our Lady arrives. This is very important. God, the Lord, has a Mother and in his Mother we truly recognize God's motherly goodness. Our Lady, Mother of God, is the Help of Christians, she is our permanent comfort, our great help. I see this too in the dialogue with the bishops of the world, of Africa and lately also of Latin America; I see that love for Our Lady is the driving force of catholicity. In Our Lady we recognize all God's tenderness, so, fostering and living out Our

Lady's, Mary's, joyful love is a very great gift of catholicity.

Then there are the saints. Every place has its own saint. This is good because in this way we see the range of colours of God's one light and of his love which comes close to us. It means discovering the saints in their beauty, in their drawing close to me in the Word, so that in a specific saint I may find expressed precisely for me the inexhaustible Word of God, and then all the aspects of parochial life, even the human ones. We must not always be in the clouds, in the loftiest clouds of Mystery. We must have our feet firmly planted on the ground and together live the joy of being a great family: the great little family of the parish; the great family of the diocese, the great family of the universal Church. In Rome I can see all this, I can see how people from every part of the world who do not know one another are actually acquainted because they all belong to the family of God. They are close to one another because they all possess the love of the Lord, the love of Our Lady, the love of the saints, Apostolic Succession and the Successor of Peter and the Bishops.

I would say that this joy of catholicity with its many different hues is also the joy of beauty. We have here the beauty of a beautiful organ; the beauty of a very beautiful church, the beauty that has developed in the Church. I think this is a marvellous testimony of God's presence and of the truth of God. Truth is expressed in beauty, and we must be grateful for this beauty and seek to do our utmost to ensure that it is ever present, that it develops and continues to grow. In this way, I believe that God will be very concretely in our midst.

I am Fr Lorenzo, a parish priest. Holy Father, the faithful expect only one thing from priests: that they be experts in encouraging the encounter of human beings with God. These are not my own words but something Your Holiness said in an Address to the clergy. My spiritual director at the seminary, in those trying sessions of spiritual direction, said to me: 'Lorenzino, humanly we've made it, but. . .', and when he said 'but', what he meant was that I preferred playing football to Eucharistic Adoration. And he meant that this did my vocation no good and that it was not right to dispute lessons of morals and law, because the teachers knew more about them that I did. And with that 'but', who knows what else he meant. I now think of him in Heaven, and in any case I say some requiems for him. In spite of everything, I have been a priest for 34 years and I am happy about that, too. I have worked no miracles nor have I known any disasters or perhaps I did not recognize them. I feel that 'humanly we've made it' is a great compliment. However, does not bringing man close to God and God to man pass above all through what we call humanity, which is indispensable even for us priests?

Pope Benedict XVI: Thank you. I would simply say 'yes' to what you said at the end. Catholicism, somewhat simplistically, has always been considered the religion of the great '*et et*':[23] not of great forms of exclusivism but of synthesis. The exact meaning of 'Catholic' is 'synthesis'. I would therefore be against having to choose between either playing football or studying Sacred Scripture or Canon Law. Let us do both these things. It is great to do sports. I am not a great sportsman, yet I used to like going to the mountains when I was younger; now I only go on some very easy excursions, but I always find it very beautiful to walk here in this wonderful earth that the Lord has given to us. Therefore, we cannot always live in exalted meditation; perhaps a saint on the last step of his earthly pilgrimage could reach this point, but we normally live with our feet on the ground and our eyes turned to Heaven. Both these things are given to us by the Lord and therefore loving human things, loving the beauties of this earth, is not only very human but also very Christian and truly Catholic.

---

23. *both . . . and . . .*

I would say – and it seems to me that I have already mentioned this earlier – that this aspect is also part of a good and truly Catholic pastoral care: living in the *'et et'*; living the humanity and humanism of the human being, all the gifts which the Lord has lavished upon us and which we have developed; and at the same time, not forgetting God, because ultimately, the great light comes from God and then it is only from him that comes the light which gives joy to all these aspects of the things that exist. Therefore, I would simply like to commit myself to the great Catholic synthesis, to this *'et et'*; to be truly human. And each person, in accordance with his or her own gifts and charism, should not only love the earth and the beautiful things the Lord has given us, but also be grateful because God's light shines on earth and bathes everything in splendour and beauty. In this regard, let us live catholicity joyfully. This would be my answer.

I am Fr Arnaldo. Holy Father, pastoral and ministerial requirements in addition to the reduced number of priests impel our bishops to review the distribution of clergy, resulting in an accumulation of tasks for one priest as well as responsibility for more than one parish. This closely affects many communities of the baptized and requires that we priests – priests and lay people – live and exercise the pastoral ministry together. How is it possible to live this change in pastoral organization, giving priority to the spirituality of the Good Shepherd? Thank you, Your Holiness.

Pope Benedict XVI: Yes, let us return to this question of pastoral priorities and how to be a parish priest today. A little while ago, a French bishop who was a religious and so had never been a parish priest, said to me: 'Your Holiness, I would like you to explain to me what a parish priest is. In France we have these large pastoral units covering five, six or seven parishes and the parish priest becomes a coordinator of bodies, of different initiatives.' But it seemed to him, since he was so busy coordinating the different bodies he was obliged to deal with, that he no longer had the possibility of a personal encounter with his sheep. Since he was a bishop, hence, the pastor of a large parish, he wondered if this system were right or whether we ought to rediscover a possibility for the parish priest to be truly a parish priest, hence, pastor of his flock. I could not, of course, come up with the recipe for an instant solution to the situation in France, but the problem in general is: to ensure that, despite the new situations and new forms of responsibility, the parish priest does not forfeit his closeness to the people, his truly being in person the shepherd of this flock entrusted to him by the Lord.

Situations are not the same: I am thinking of the bishops in their dioceses with widely differing situations; they must see clearly how to ensure that the parish priest continues to be a pastor and does not become a holy bureaucrat. In any case, I think that a first opportunity in which we can be present for the people entrusted to us is precisely the sacramental life. In the Eucharist we are together and can and must meet one another; the Sacrament of Penance and Reconciliation is a very personal encounter; Baptism is a personal encounter and not only the moment of the conferral of the Sacrament.

I would say that all these sacraments have a context of their own: baptizing entails offering the young family a little catechesis, speaking to them so that Baptism may also become a personal encounter and an opportunity for a very concrete catechesis. Preparation for First Communion, Confirmation and Marriage is likewise always an opportunity for the parish priest, the priest, to meet people personally; he is the preacher and administrator of the sacraments in a way that always involves the human dimension. A sacrament is never merely a ritual act, but the ritual and sacramental act strengthens the human context in which the priest or parish priest acts.

Furthermore, I think it very important to find the right ways to delegate. It is not right that the parish priest should only coordinate other bodies. Rather, he should delegate in various ways, and obviously at Synods – and here in this diocese you have had the Synod – a way is found to free the parish priest sufficiently. This should be done in such a way that on the one hand he retains responsibility for the totality of pastoral units entrusted to him. He should not be reduced to being mainly and above all a coordinating bureaucrat. On the contrary, he should be the one who holds the essential reins himself but can also rely on collaborators. I believe that this is one of the important and positive results of the Council: the co-responsibility of the entire parish, for the parish priest is no longer the only one to animate everything. Since we all form a parish together, we must all collaborate and help so that the parish priest is not left on his own, mainly as a coordinator, but truly discovers that he is a pastor who is backed up in these common tasks in which, together, the parish lives and is fulfilled. Thus, I would say that, on the one hand, this coordination and vital responsibility for the whole parish, and on the other, the sacramental life and preaching as a centre of parish life, could also today, in circumstances which are of course more difficult, make it possible to be a parish priest who may not know each person by name, as the Lord says of the Good Shepherd, but one who really knows his sheep and is really their pastor who calls and guides them.

APOSTOLIC JOURNEY OF HIS HOLINESS
BENEDICT XVI TO AUSTRIA ON THE
OCCASION OF THE 850th ANNIVERSARY
OF THE FOUNDATION OF THE SHRINE
OF MARIAZELL

THE ADDRESS GIVEN AT VESPERS WITH PRIESTS, RELIGIOUS, DEACONS AND SEMINARIANS

Shrine of Mariazell
Saturday, 8 September 2007

Poverty, Chastity & Obedience

We have come together in the venerable Basilica of our *Magna Mater Austriae* in Mariazell. For many generations people have come to pray here to obtain the help of the Mother of God. We too are doing the same today. We want to join Mary in praising God's immense goodness and in expressing our gratitude to the Lord for all the blessings we have received, especially the great gift of the faith. We also wish to commend to Mary our heartfelt concerns: to beg her protection for the Church, to invoke her intercession for the gift of worthy vocations for dioceses and religious communities, to implore her assistance for families and her merciful prayers for all those longing for freedom from sin and for the grace of conversion, and, finally, to entrust to Mary's maternal care our sick and our elderly. May the great Mother of Austria and of Europe bring all of us to a profound renewal of faith and life!

Dear friends, as priests, and as men and women religious, you are servants of the mission of Jesus Christ. Just as two thousand years ago Jesus called people to follow him, today too young men and women are setting out at his call, attracted by him and moved by a desire to devote their lives to serving the Church and helping others. They have the courage to follow Christ, and they want to be his witnesses. Being a follower of Christ is full of risks, since we are constantly threatened by sin, lack of freedom and defection. Consequently, we all need his grace, just as Mary received it in its fullness. We learn to look always, like Mary, to Christ, and to make him our criterion and measure. Thus we can participate in the universal saving mission of the Church, of which he is the head. The Lord calls priests, religious and lay people to go into the world, in all its complexity, and to cooperate in the building up of God's Kingdom. They do this in a great variety of ways: in preaching, in building communities, in the different pastoral ministries, in the practical exercise of charity, in research and scientific study carried out in an apostolic spirit, in dialogue with the surrounding culture, in promoting the justice willed by God and, in no less measure, in the recollected contemplation of the triune God and the common praise of God in their communities.

The Lord invites you to join the Church 'on her pilgrim way through history'. He is inviting you to become pilgrims with him and to share in his life which today too includes both the way of the Cross and the way of the Risen One through the Galilee of our existence. But he remains always one and the same Lord who, through the one Baptism, calls us to the one faith. Taking part in his journey thus means both things: the dimension of the Cross – with failure, suffering, misunderstanding and even contempt and persecution – but also the experience of profound joy in his service and of the great consolation born of an encounter with him. Like the Church, individual parishes, communities and all baptized Christians find in their experience of the crucified and risen Christ the source of their mission.

At the heart of the mission of Jesus Christ and of every Christian is the proclamation of the Kingdom of God. Proclaiming the Kingdom in the name of Christ means for the Church, for priests, men and women religious, and for all the baptized, a commitment to be present in the world as his witnesses. The Kingdom of God is really God himself, who makes himself present in our midst and reigns through us. The Kingdom of God is built up when God lives in us and we bring God into the world. You do so when you testify to a 'meaning' rooted in God's creative love and opposed to every kind of meaninglessness and despair. You stand alongside all those who are earnestly striving to discover this meaning, alongside all those who want to make something positive of their lives. By your prayer and intercession, you are the advocates of all who seek God, who are journeying towards God. You bear witness to a hope which, against every form of hopelessness, silent or spoken, points to the fidelity and the loving concern of God. Hence you are on the side of those who are crushed by misfortune and cannot break free of their burdens. You bear witness to that Love which gives itself for humanity and thus conquered death. You are on the side of all who have never known love, and who are no longer able to believe in life. And so you stand against all forms of injustice, hidden or apparent, and against a growing contempt for man. In this way, dear brothers and sisters, your whole life needs to be, like that of John the Baptist, a great, living witness to Jesus Christ, the Son of God incarnate. Jesus called John 'a burning and shining lamp' (Jn 5: 35). You too must be such lamps! Let your light shine in our society, in political and economic life, in culture and research. Even if it is only a flicker amid so many deceptive lights, it nonetheless draws its power and splendour from the great Morning Star, the Risen Christ, whose light shines brilliantly – wants to shine brilliantly through us – and will never fade.

Following Christ – we want to follow him – following Christ means taking on ever more fully his mind and his way of life; this is what the Letter to the Philippians tells us: 'Let the same mind be in you that was in Christ!' (cf. 2: 5). 'To Look to Christ' is the theme of these days. In looking to him, the great Teacher of life, the Church has discerned three striking features of Jesus' basic attitude. These three features – with the Tradition we call them the 'evangelical counsels' – have become the distinctive elements of a life committed to the radical following of Christ: poverty, chastity and obedience. Let us reflect now briefly on them.

Jesus Christ, who was rich with the very richness of God, became poor for our sake, as Saint Paul tells us in the Second Letter to the Corinthians (cf. 8: 9); this is an unfathomable statement, one to which we should always return for further reflection. And in the Letter to the Philippians we read: He emptied himself; he humbled himself and became obedient even to death on a Cross (cf. 2: 6ff.) The one who himself became poor, called the poor 'blessed'. Saint Luke, in his version of the Beatitudes, makes us understand that this statement – calling the poor blessed – certainly refers to the poor, the truly poor, in Israel at that time, where a sharp distinction existed between rich and poor. But Saint Matthew, in his version of the Beatitudes, explains to us that material poverty alone is not enough to ensure God's closeness, since the heart can be hard and filled with lust for riches. Matthew – like all of Scripture – lets us understand that in any case God is particularly close to the poor. So it becomes evident: in the poor Christians see the Christ who awaits them, who awaits their commitment. Anyone who wants to follow Christ in a radical way must renounce material goods. But he or she must live this poverty in a way centred on Christ, as a means of becoming inwardly free for their neighbour. For all Christians, but especially for us priests, and for religious, both as individuals and in community, the issue of poverty and the poor must be the object of a constant and serious examination of conscience. In our own situation, in which we are not badly off, we are not poor, I think that we ought to reflect particularly on how we can live out this calling in a sincere way. I would like to recommend it for your – for our – examination of conscience.

To understand correctly the meaning of chastity, we must start with its positive content. Once again, we find this only by looking to Christ. Jesus' life had a two-fold direction: he lived for the Father and for others. In sacred Scripture we see Jesus as a man of prayer, one who spends entire nights in dialogue with the Father. Through his prayer, he made his own humanity, and the humanity of us all, part of his filial relation to the Father. This dialogue with the Father thus became a constantly-renewed mission to the world, to us. Jesus' mission led him to a pure and unreserved commitment to men and women. Sacred Scripture shows that at no moment of his life did he betray even the slightest trace of self-interest or selfishness in his relationship with others. Jesus loved others in the Father, starting from the Father – and thus he loved them in their true being, in their reality. Entering into these sentiments of Jesus Christ – in this total communion with the living God and in this completely pure communion with others, unreservedly at their disposition – this entering into the mind of Christ inspired in Paul a theology and a way of life consonant with Jesus' words about celibacy for the Kingdom of heaven (cf. Mt 19: 12). Priests and religious are not aloof from interpersonal relationships. Chastity, on the contrary, means – and this is where I wished to start – an intense relationship; it is, positively speaking, a relationship with the living Christ and, on the basis of that, with the Father. Consequently, by the vow of celibate chastity we do not consecrate ourselves to individualism or a life of isolation; instead, we solemnly promise to put completely and unreservedly at the service of God's Kingdom – and thus at the service of others – the deep relationships of which we are capable and which we receive as a gift. In this way priests and religious become men and women of hope: staking everything on God and thus showing that God for them is something real, they open up a space for his presence – the presence of God's Kingdom – in our world. Dear priests and religious, you have an important contribution to make: amid so much greed, possessiveness, consumerism and the cult of the individual, we strive to show selfless love for men and women. We are living lives of hope, a hope whose fulfilment we leave in God's hands, because we believe that he will fulfil it. What might have happened had the history of Christianity lacked such outstanding figures and examples? What would our world be like, if there were no priests, if there were no men and women in religious congregations and communities of consecrated life – people whose lives testify to the hope of a fulfilment beyond every human desire and an experience of the love of God which transcends all human love? Precisely today, the world needs our witness.

We now come to obedience. Jesus lived his entire life, from the hidden years in Nazareth to the very moment of his death on the Cross in listening to the Father, in obedience to the Father. We see this in an exemplary way at Gethsemane. 'Not my will, but yours be done.' In this prayer Jesus takes up into his filial will the stubborn resistance of us all, and transforms our rebelliousness into his obedience. Jesus was a man of prayer. But at the same time he was also someone who knew how to listen and to obey: he became 'obedient unto death, even death on a cross' (Phil 2: 8). Christians have always known from experience that, in abandoning themselves to the will of the Father, they lose nothing, but instead discover in this way their deepest identity and interior freedom. In Jesus they have discovered that those who lose themselves find themselves, and those who bind themselves in an obedience grounded in God and inspired by the search for God, become free. Listening to God and obeying him has nothing to do with external constraint and the loss of oneself. Only by entering into God's will do we attain our true identity. Our world today needs the testimony of this experience precisely because of its desire for 'self-realization' and 'self-determination'.

Romano Guardini relates in his autobiography how, at a critical moment on his journey, when the faith of his childhood was shaken, the fundamental decision of his entire life – his conversion – came to him through an encounter with the saying of Jesus that only the one who loses himself finds himself (cf. Mk 8: 34ff.; Jn 12: 25); without self-surrender, without self-loss, there can be no self-discovery or self-realization. But then the question arose: to what extent is it proper to lose myself? To whom can I give myself? It became clear to him that we can surrender ourselves completely only if by doing so we fall into the hands of God. Only in him, in the end, can we lose ourselves and only in him can we find ourselves. But then the question arose: Who is God? Where is God? Then he came to understand that the God to whom we can surrender ourselves is alone the God who became tangible and close to us in Jesus Christ. But once more the question arose: Where do I find Jesus Christ? How can I truly give myself to him? The answer Guardini found after much searching was this: Jesus is concretely present to us only in his Body, the Church. As a result, obedience to God's will, obedience to Jesus Christ, must be, really and practically, humble obedience to the Church. I think that this too is something calling us to a constant and deep examination of conscience. It is all summed up in the prayer of Saint Ignatius of Loyola – a prayer which always seems to me so overwhelming that I am almost afraid to say it, yet one which, for all its difficulty, we should always repeat: 'Take O Lord, and receive all my liberty, my memory, my understanding and my entire will. All that I have and all that I possess you have given me: I surrender it all to you; it is all yours, dispose of it according to your will. Give me only your love and your grace; with these I will be rich enough and will desire nothing more.'

Dear brothers and sisters! You are about to return to those places where you live and carry out your ecclesial, pastoral, spiritual and human activity. May Mary, our great Advocate and Mother, watch over and protect you and your work. May she intercede for you with her Son, our Lord Jesus Christ. I thank you for your prayers and your labours in the Lord's vineyard, and I join you in praying that God will protect and bless all of you, and everyone, particularly the young people, both here in Austria and in the various countries from which many of you have come. With affection I accompany all of you with my blessing.

APOSTOLIC JOURNEY OF HIS HOLINESS
BENEDICT XVI TO AUSTRIA ON THE
OCCASION OF THE 850th ANNIVERSARY
OF THE FOUNDATION OF THE SHRINE
OF MARIAZELL

THE ADDRESS GIVEN FOR THE PAPAL VISIT TO HEILIGENKREUZ ABBEY

Sunday, 9 September 2007

The Divine Office

On my pilgrimage to the *Magna Mater Austriae*, I am pleased to visit this Abbey of Heiligenkreuz, which is not only an important stop on the *Via Sacra* leading to Mariazell, but the oldest continuously active Cistercian monastery in the world. I wished to come to this place so rich in history in order to draw attention to the fundamental directive of Saint Benedict, according to whose Rule Cistercians also live. Quite simply, Benedict insisted that 'nothing be put before the divine Office.'[24]

For this reason, in a monastery of Benedictine spirit, the praise of God, which the monks sing as a solemn choral prayer, always has priority. Monks are certainly – thank God! – not the only people who pray; others also pray: children, the young and the old, men and women, the married and the single – all Christians

---

24. *Regula Benedicti* 43,3.

pray, or at least, they should!

In the life of monks, however, prayer takes on a particular importance: it is the heart of their calling. Their vocation is to be men of prayer. In the patristic period the monastic life was likened to the life of the angels. It was considered the essential mark of the angels that they are worshippers. Their very life is worship. This should hold true also for monks. Monks pray first and foremost not for any specific intention, but simply because God is worthy of being praised. '*Confitemini Domino, quoniam bonus!* – Praise the Lord, for he is good, for his mercy is eternal!': so we are urged by a number of Psalms (e.g. Ps 106: 1). Such prayer for its own sake, intended as pure divine service, is rightly called *officium*. It is 'service' par excellence, the 'sacred service' of monks. It is offered to the triune God who, above all else, is worthy 'to receive glory, honour and power' (Rev 4: 11), because he wondrously created the world and even more wondrously renewed it.

At the same time, the *officium* of consecrated persons is also a sacred service to men and women, a testimony offered to them. All people have deep within their hearts, whether they know it or not, a yearning for definitive fulfilment, for supreme happiness, and thus, ultimately, for God. A monastery, in which the community gathers several times a day for the praise of God, testifies to the fact that this primordial human longing does not go unfulfilled: God the Creator has not placed us in a fearful darkness where, groping our way in despair, we seek some ultimate meaning (cf. Acts 17: 27); God has not abandoned us in a desert void, bereft of meaning, where in the end only death awaits us. No! God has shone forth in our darkness with his light, with his Son Jesus Christ. In him, God has entered our world in all his 'fullness' (cf. Col 1: 19); in him all truth, the truth for which we yearn, has its source and summit.[25]

---

25. Cf. Second Vatican Ecumenical Council, *Gaudium et Spes*, 22.

Our light, our truth, our goal, our fulfilment, our life – all this is not a religious doctrine but a person: *Jesus Christ*. Over and above any ability of our own to seek and to desire God, we ourselves were already sought and desired, and indeed, found and redeemed by him! The gaze of people of every time and nation, of all the philosophies, religions and cultures, ultimately encounters the wide open eyes of the crucified and risen Son of God; his open heart is the fullness of love. The eyes of Christ are the eyes of a loving God. The image of the Crucified Lord above the altar, whose romanesque original is found in the Cathedral of Sarzano, shows that this gaze is turned to every man and woman. The Lord, in truth, looks into the hearts of each of us.

The core of monasticism is worship – living like the angels. But since monks are people of flesh and blood on this earth, Saint Benedict added to the central command: *'pray'*, a second command: *'work'*. In the mind of Saint Benedict, and Saint Bernard as well, part of monastic life, along with prayer, is work: the cultivation of the land in accordance with the Creator's will. Thus in every age monks, setting out from their gaze upon God, have made the earth life-giving and lovely. Their protection and renewal of creation derived precisely from their looking to God. In the rhythm of the *ora et labora*,[26] the community of consecrated persons bears witness to the God who, in Jesus Christ, looks upon us, while human beings and the world, as God looks upon them, become good.

Monks are not the only ones who pray the *officium*; from the monastic tradition the Church has derived the obligation for all religious, and also for priests and deacons, to recite the Breviary. Here too, it is appropriate for men and women religious, priests and deacons – and naturally bishops as well – to come before God in their daily 'official' prayer with hymns and psalms, with

---

26. *Prayer and work.*

thanksgiving and pure petition.

Dear brother priests and deacons, dear brothers and sisters in the consecrated life! I realize that discipline is needed, and sometimes great effort as well, in order to recite the Breviary faithfully; but through this *officium* we also receive many riches: how many times, in doing so, have we seen our weariness and despondency melt away! When God is faithfully praised and worshipped, his blessings are unfailing. In Austria, people rightly say: 'Everything depends on God's blessing!'

Your primary service to this world must therefore be your prayer and the celebration of the divine Office. The interior disposition of each priest, and of each consecrated person, must be that of 'putting nothing before the divine Office'. The beauty of this inner attitude will find expression in the beauty of the liturgy, so that wherever we join in singing, praising, exalting and worshipping God, a little bit of heaven will become present on earth. Truly it would not be presumptuous to say that, in a liturgy completely centred on God, we can see, in its rituals and chant, an image of eternity. Otherwise, how could our forefathers, hundreds of years ago, have built a sacred edifice as solemn as this? Here the architecture itself draws all our senses upwards, towards 'what eye has not seen, nor ear heard, nor the heart of man imagined: what God has prepared for those who love him' (I Cor 2: 9). In all our efforts on behalf of the liturgy, the determining factor must always be our looking to God. We stand before God – he speaks to us and we speak to him. Whenever in our thinking we are only concerned about making the liturgy attractive, interesting and beautiful, the battle is already lost. Either it is *Opus Dei*,[27] with God as its specific subject, or it is not. In the light of this, I ask you to celebrate the sacred liturgy with your gaze fixed on God within the communion of saints,

---

27. *Work of God.*

the living Church of every time and place, so that it will truly be an expression of the sublime beauty of the God who has called men and women to be his friends!

The soul of prayer, ultimately, is the Holy Spirit. Whenever we pray, it is he who 'helps us in our weakness, interceding for us with sighs too deep for words' (Rom 8: 26). Trusting in these words of the Apostle Paul, I assure you, dear brothers and sisters, that prayer will produce in you the same effect which once led to the custom of calling priests and consecrated persons simply 'spirituals' (*Geistliche*). Bishop Sailer of Regensburg once said that priests should be first and foremost spiritual persons. I would like to see a revival of the word '*Geistliche*'. More importantly, though, the content of that word should become a part of our lives: namely, that in following the Lord, we become, by the power of the Spirit, 'spiritual' men and women.

Austria (*Österreich*) is, in an old play on words, truly *Klösterreich*: a realm of monasteries and a land rich in monasteries. Your ancient abbeys whose origins and traditions date back many centuries are places where 'God is put first'. Dear friends, make this priority given to God very apparent to people! As a spiritual oasis, a monastery reminds today's world of the most important, and indeed, in the end, the only decisive thing: that there is an ultimate reason why life is worth living: God and his unfathomable love.

And I ask you, dear members of the faithful: see your abbeys and monasteries for what they are and always wish to be: not mere strongholds of culture and tradition, or even simple business enterprises. Structure, organization and finances are necessary in the Church too, but they are not what is essential. A monastery is above all this: a place of spiritual power. Coming to one of your monasteries here in Austria, we have the same impression as when, after a strenuous hike in the Alps, we finally find refreshment at a clear mountain spring. . . . Take advantage of these springs of God's closeness in your country; treasure the religious communities, the monasteries and abbeys; and make use of the spiritual service that consecrated person are willing to offer you!

Finally, I have come also to visit the Academy, now the Pontifical Academy, which is 205 years old and which, in its new status, the Abbot has named after the present Successor of Peter. Important though it is that the discipline of theology be part of the *universitas*[28] of knowledge through the presence of Catholic theological faculties in state universities, it is equally important that there should be academic institutions like your own, where there can be a deeper interplay between scientific theology and lived spirituality. God is never simply the 'object' of theology; he is always its living 'subject' as well. Christian theology, for that matter, is never a purely human discourse about God, but always, and inseparably, the *logos* and 'logic' of God's self-revelation. For this reason scientific rationality and lived devotion are two necessarily complementary and interdependent aspects of study.

The father of the Cistercian Order, Saint Bernard, in his own day fought against the detachment of an objectivizing rationality from the main current of ecclesial spirituality. Our situation today, while different, nonetheless has notable similarities. In its desire to be recognized as a rigorously scientific discipline in the modern sense, theology can lose the life-breath given by faith. But just as a liturgy which no longer looks to God is already in its death throes, so too a theology which no longer draws its life-breath from faith ceases to be theology; it ends up as a array of more or less loosely connected disciplines. But where theology is practised 'on bent knee', as Hans Urs von Balthasar urged, it will prove fruitful for the Church in Austria and beyond.[29]

---

28. *The whole.*
29. Cf. Hans Urs von Balthasar, 'Theologie und Heiligkeit', an essay written in 1948, in *Verbum Caro. Skizzen zur Theologie I*, Einsiedeln, 1960, 195-224.

This fruitfulness is shown through fostering and forming those who have vocations to the priesthood or the religious life. Today, if such a vocation is to be sustained faithfully over a lifetime, there is a need for a formation capable of integrating faith and reason, heart and mind, life and thought. A life devoted to following Christ calls for an integration of one's entire personality. Neglect of the intellectual dimension can give rise all too easily to a kind of superficial piety nourished mostly by emotions and sentiments, which cannot be sustained over a lifetime. Neglect of the spiritual dimension, in turn, can create a rarified rationalism which, in its coldness and detachment, can never bring about an enthusiastic self-surrender to God. A life devoted to following Christ cannot be built on such one-sided foundations; half-measures leave a person unhappy and, consequently, also spiritually barren. Each vocation to the religious life or to the priesthood is a treasure so precious that those responsible for it should do everything possible to ensure a formation which promotes both *fides et ratio* – faith and reason, heart and mind.

Saint Leopold of Austria . . . on the advice of his son, Blessed Otto of Freising, who was my predecessor in the episcopal see of Freising (his feast is celebrated today in Freising), founded your abbey in 1133, and called it *Unsere Liebe Frau zum Heiligen Kreuz* – Our Lady of Holy Cross. This monastery is dedicated to Our Lady not simply by tradition – like every Cistercian monastery – but among you there burns the Marian flame of Saint Bernard of Clairvaux. Bernard, who entered the monastery along with thirty of his companions, is a kind of patron saint of vocations. Perhaps it was because of his particular devotion to Our Lady that he exercised such a compelling and infectious influence on his many young contemporaries called by God. Where Mary is, there is the archetype of total self-giving and Christian discipleship. Where Mary is, there is the pentecostal breath of the Holy Spirit; there is new beginning and authentic renewal.

From this Marian sanctuary on the *Via Sacra*, I pray that all Austria's shrines will experience fruitfulness and further growth. Here, as at Mariazell, I would like, before leaving, to ask the Mother of God once more to intercede for all of Austria. In the words of Saint Bernard, I invite everyone to become a trusting child before Mary, even as the Son of God did. Saint Bernard says, and we say with him: 'Look to the star of the sea, call upon Mary . . . in danger, in distress, in doubt, think of Mary, call upon Mary. May her name never be far from your lips, or far from your heart . . . If you follow her, you will not stray; if you pray to her, you will not despair; if you turn your thoughts to her, you will not err. If she holds you, you will not fall; if she protects you, you need not fear; if she is your guide, you will not tire; if she is gracious to you, you will surely reach your destination.'[30]

---

30. Bernard of Clairvaux, *In laudibus Virginis Matris*, Homilia 2, 17.

From the

ADDRESS TO THE BISHOPS OF KENYA ON THEIR 'AD LIMINA' VISIT

Consistory Hall
Monday, 19 November 2007

'A prayer in communion with Jesus Christ'

Within each diocese, the vibrancy and harmony of the presbyterate offers a clear sign of the vitality of the local Church. Structures of consultation and participation are necessary, but can be ineffective if the proper spirit is missing. As bishops, we must constantly strive to build up the sense of community among our priests, united in the love of Christ and in their sacramental ministry. Life can be difficult for priests today. They can feel isolated or alone and overwhelmed by their pastoral responsibilities. We must be close to them and encourage them, in the first place, to remain firmly rooted in prayer, because only those who are themselves nourished are able to nourish others in turn. Let them drink deeply from the wells of Sacred Scripture and from the daily and reverent celebration of the most holy Eucharist. Let them give themselves generously to praying the Liturgy of the Hours, a prayer that is made 'in communion with all who pray throughout history, a prayer in communion with Jesus Christ' (*Address to the priests and permanent deacons of Bavaria*, 14 September 2006). By praying in this way they include and represent others who may lack the time or energy or capacity to pray, and thus the power of prayer, the presence of Jesus Christ, renews their priesthood and flows out into the world (cf. ibid.). Help your priests in this way to grow in solidarity with one another, with their people, and with you, as your consecrated co-workers. Respectful dialogue and closeness between bishop and priests not only builds up the local Church but also edifies the entire community. Indeed, visible unity among the spiritual leaders can be a powerful antidote against division within the wider family of God's people.

From the

ADDRESS GIVEN DURING A MEETING WITH THE PARISH PRIESTS AND THE CLERGY OF THE DIOCESE OF ROME

Hall of Blessings
Thursday, 7 February 2008

'I am also a deacon'

Every priest, of course, also continues to be a deacon and must always be aware of this dimension, for the Lord himself became our minister, our deacon. Recall the act of the washing of the feet, where it is explicitly shown that the Teacher, the Lord, acts as a deacon and wants those who follow him to be deacons and carry out this ministry for humanity, to the point that they even help us to wash the dirty feet of the people entrusted to our care. This dimension seems to me to be of paramount importance.

On this occasion a small experience noted by Paul VI springs to mind – although it may not be quite relevant to our subject. Every day of the Council the Gospel was enthroned. The Pontiff once told the masters of ceremonies that he himself would like to be the one who enthroned the Gospel. They said: No, this is a task for deacons and not for the Pope, the Supreme Pontiff, or the bishops. He noted in his diary: But I am also a deacon, I am still a deacon, and I too would like to exercise my diaconal ministry by enthroning the Word of God. Thus, this concerns us all. Priests remain deacons and deacons clarify this diaconal dimension of our ministry in the Church and in the world. The liturgical enthronement of the Word of God every day during the Council was always an act of great importance: it told us who was the true Lord of that Assembly, it told us that the Word of God is on the throne and that we exercise the ministry to listen to and interpret this Word in order to offer it to others. To enthrone the Word of God, the living Word or Christ, in the world underlies the meaning of all we do. May it truly be he who governs our personal life and our life in the parishes.

'We must also speak of sin itself'

In the Encyclical *Spe Salvi* I wanted to speak precisely about the Last Judgement, judgement in general, and in this context also about Purgatory, Hell and Heaven. I think we have all been struck by the Marxist objection that Christians have only spoken of the afterlife and have ignored the earth. Thus, we demonstrate that we are truly committed to our earth and are not people who talk about distant realties, who do not help the earth. Now, although it is right to show that Christians work for the earth – and we are all called to work to make this earth really a city for God and of God – we must not forget the other dimension. Unless we take it into account, we cannot work well for the earth: to show this was one of my fundamental purposes in writing the encyclical. When one does not know the judgement of God one does not know the possibility of Hell, of the radical and definitive failure of life, one does not know the possibility of and need for purification. Man then fails to work well for the earth because he ultimately loses his criteria, he no longer knows himself – through not knowing God – and destroys the earth. All the great ideologies have promised: we will take things in hand, we will no longer neglect the earth, we will create a new, just, correct and brotherly world. But they destroyed the world instead. We see it with Nazism, we also see it with Communism which promised to build the world as it was supposed to be and instead destroyed it.

In the *ad limina* visits of bishops from former Communist countries, I always see anew that in those lands, not only the planet and ecology, but above all and more seriously, souls have been destroyed. Rediscovering the truly human conscience illuminated by God's presence is our first task for the re-edification of the earth. This is the common experience of those countries. The re-edification of the earth, while respecting this planet's cry of suffering, can only be achieved by rediscovering God in the soul with the eyes open to God.

We must speak of all this precisely because of our responsibility to the earth, to the people who are alive today. We must also speak of sin itself as the possibility of destroying ourselves, hence, also other parts of the world. In the encyclical I tried to show that it is God's Last Judgement that guarantees justice. We all want a just world. Yet we cannot atone for all the destruction of the past, all the people unjustly tortured and killed. God alone can create justice, which must be justice for all, even for the dead, and as the great Marxist Adorno said, only the resurrection of the body, which he claimed as unreal, would be able to create justice. We believe in this resurrection of the body in which not all will be equal. Today people have become used to thinking: what is sin? God is great, he knows us, so sin does not count; in the end God will be kind to us all. It is a beautiful hope. But both justice and true guilt exist. Those who have destroyed man and the earth cannot suddenly sit down at God's table together with their victims. God creates justice. We must keep this in mind.

Therefore, I felt it was important to write this text also about Purgatory, which for me is an obvious truth, so evident and also so necessary and comforting that it could not be absent. I tried to say: perhaps those who have destroyed themselves in this way, who are for ever unredeemable, who no longer possess any elements on which God's love can rest, who no longer have a minimal capacity for loving, may not be so numerous. This would be Hell. On the other hand, those who are so pure that they can enter immediately into God's communion are undoubtedly few – or at any rate not many. A great many of us hope that there is something in us that can be saved, that there may be in us a final desire to serve God and serve human beings, to live in accordance with God. Yet there are so very many wounds, there is so much filth. We need to be prepared, to be purified. This is our hope: even with so much dirt in our souls, in the end the Lord will give us the possibility, he will wash us at last with his goodness that comes from his Cross. In this way he makes us capable of being for him in eternity. And thus Heaven is hope, it is justice brought about at last.

He also gives us criteria by which to live, so that this time may be in some way paradise, a first gleam of paradise. Where people live according to these criteria a hint of paradise appears in the world and is visible. It also seems to me to be a demonstration of the truth of faith, of the need to follow the road of the Commandments, of which we must speak further. These really are road signs on our way and show us how to live well, how to choose life. Therefore, we must also speak of sin and of the sacrament of forgiveness and reconciliation. A sincere person knows that he is guilty, that he must start again, that he must be purified. And this is the marvellous reality which the Lord offers us: there is a chance of renewal, of being new. The Lord starts with us again and in this way we can also start again with the others in our life.

This aspect of renewal, of the restitution of our being after so many errors, so many sins, is the great promise, the great gift the Church offers but which psychotherapy, for example, cannot offer. Today, in the face of so many destroyed or seriously injured psyches, psychotherapy is so widespread and also necessary. Yet the possibilities of psychotherapy are very limited: it can only make some sort of effort to restore balance to an unbalanced soul but cannot provide true renewal, the overcoming of these serious diseases of the soul. It is therefore always temporary and never definitive. The Sacrament of Penance gives us the opportunity to be renewed through and through with God's power – *ego te absolvo*[31] – which is possible because Christ took these sins, this guilt, upon himself. I think there is a great need of this especially today. We can be healed. Souls that are wounded and ill, as everyone knows by experience, not only need advice but true renewal, which can only come from God's power, from the power of Crucified Love. I feel this is the important connection of the mysteries which in the end truly affect our lives. We must recover them ourselves and so bring them once again within our people's reach.

31. The words of Sacramental absolution, 'I absolve you'.

From the

ADDRESS TO THE PARTICIPANTS IN A COURSE ON THE INTERNAL FORUM ORGANIZED BY THE TRIBUNAL OF THE APOSTOLIC PENITENTIARY

Hall of Blessings
Friday, 7 March 2008

'The soothing joy of God's forgiveness'

Lent is an especially favourable season to meditate on the reality of sin in the light of God's infinite mercy, which the Sacrament of Penance expresses in its loftiest form. I therefore willingly take this opportunity to bring to your attention certain thoughts on the administration of this Sacrament in our time, in which the loss of the sense of sin is unfortunately becoming increasingly more widespread. It is necessary today to assist those who confess to experience that divine tenderness to repentant sinners which many Gospel episodes portray with tones of deep feeling. Let us take, for example, the passage in Luke's Gospel that presents the woman who was a sinner and was forgiven (cf. Lk 7: 36-50). Simon, a Pharisee and a rich dignitary of the town, was holding a banquet at his home in honour of Jesus. In accordance with a custom of that time, the meal was eaten with the doors left open, for in this way the fame and prestige of the homeowner was increased. All at once, an uninvited and unexpected guest entered from the back of the room: a well-known prostitute. One can understand the embarrassment of those present, which did not seem, however, to bother the woman. She came forward and somewhat furtively stopped at Jesus' feet. She had heard his words of pardon and hope for all, even prostitutes; she was moved and stayed where she was in silence. She bathed Jesus' feet with tears, wiped them dry with her hair, kissed them and anointed them with fragrant ointment. By so doing, the sinner woman wanted to express her love for and gratitude to the Lord with gestures that were familiar to her, although they were censured by society.

Amid the general embarrassment, it was Jesus himself who saved the situation: 'Simon, I have something to say to you.' 'What is it, Teacher?', the master of the house asked him. We all know Jesus' answer with a parable which we can sum up in the following words which the Lord addressed basically to Simon: 'You see? This woman knows she is a sinner; yet prompted by love, she is asking for understanding and forgiveness. You, on the other hand, presume yourself to be righteous and are perhaps convinced that you have nothing serious for which to be forgiven.'

The message that shines out from this Gospel passage is eloquent: God forgives all to those who love much. Those who trust in themselves and in their own merits are, as it were, blinded by their ego and their heart is hardened in sin. Those, on the other hand, who recognize that they are weak and sinful entrust themselves to God and obtain from him grace and forgiveness. It is precisely this message that must be transmitted: what counts most is to make people understand that in the Sacrament of Reconciliation, whatever the sin committed, if it is humbly recognized and the person involved turns with trust to the priest-confessor, he or she never fails to experience the soothing joy of God's forgiveness. In this perspective your

Course acquires considerable importance. It aims to prepare well-trained confessors from the doctrinal viewpoint who are able to make their penitents experience the Heavenly Father's merciful love. Might it not be true that today we are witnessing a certain alienation from this Sacrament? When one insists solely on the accusation of sins – which must nevertheless exist and it is necessary to help the faithful understand its importance – one risks relegating to the background what is central, that is, the personal encounter with God, the Father of goodness and mercy. It is not sin which is at the heart of the sacramental celebration but rather God's mercy, which is infinitely greater than any guilt of ours.

It must be a commitment of pastors and especially of confessors to highlight the close connection that exists between the Sacrament of Reconciliation and a life oriented decisively to conversion. It is necessary that between the practice of the Sacrament of Confession and a life in which a person strives to follow Christ sincerely, a sort of continuous 'virtuous circle' be established in which the grace of the Sacrament may sustain and nourish the commitment to be a faithful disciple of the Lord. The Lenten Season, in which we now find ourselves, reminds us that in our Christian life we must always aspire to conversion and that when we receive the Sacrament of Reconciliation frequently the desire for Gospel perfection is kept alive in believers. If this constant desire is absent, the celebration of the Sacrament unfortunately risks becoming something formal that has no effect on the fabric of daily life. If, moreover, even when one is motivated by the desire to follow Jesus one does not go regularly to confession, one risks gradually slowing his or her spiritual pace to the point of increasingly weakening and ultimately perhaps even exhausting it.

Dear brothers, it is not difficult to understand the value in the Church of your ministry as stewards of divine mercy for the salvation of souls. Persevere in imitating the example of so many holy confessors who, with their spiritual insight, helped penitents to understand that the regular celebration of the Sacrament of Penance and a Christian life that aspires to holiness are inseparable elements of the same spiritual process for every baptized person. And do not forget that you yourselves are examples of authentic Christian life. May the Virgin Mary, Mother of Mercy and of Hope, help you who are present here and all confessors to carry out zealously and joyfully this great service on which the Church's life so intensely depends. I assure you of my remembrance in prayer and bless you with affection.

APOSTOLIC JOURNEY TO THE UNITED STATES OF AMERICA AND VISIT TO THE UNITED NATIONS ORGANIZATION HEADQUARTERS

From the

INTERVIEW GIVEN DURING THE FLIGHT TO THE UNITED STATES OF AMERICA

Tuesday, 15 April 2008

'A great suffering for the Church'

Speaking of the crisis caused by sexual abuse Pope Benedict said:

It is a great suffering for the Church in the United States and for the Church in general, for me personally, that this could happen. If I read the history of these events, it is difficult for me to understand how it was possible for priests to fail in this way in the mission to give healing, to give God's love to these children. I am ashamed and we will do everything possible to ensure that this does not happen in future. I think we have to act on three levels: the first is at the level of justice and the political level. I will not speak at this moment about homosexuality: this is another thing. We will absolutely exclude paedophiles from the sacred ministry; it is absolutely incompatible, and whoever is really guilty of being a paedophile cannot be a priest. So at this first level we can do justice and help the victims, because they are deeply affected; these are the two sides of justice: one, that paedophiles cannot be priests and the other, to help in any possible way the victims. Then there is a pastoral level. The victims will need healing and help and assistance and reconciliation: this is a big pastoral engagement and I know that the bishops and the priests and all Catholic people in the United States will do whatever possible to help, to assist, to heal. We have made a visitation of the seminaries and we will do all that is possible in the education of seminarians for a deep spiritual, human and intellectual formation for the students. Only sound persons can be admitted to the priesthood and only persons with a deep personal life in Christ and who have a deep sacramental life. So, I know that the bishops and directors of seminarians will do all possible to have a strong, strong discernment because it is more important to have good priests than to have many priests. This is also our third level, and we hope that we can do, and have done and will do in the future, all that is possible to heal these wounds.

APOSTOLIC JOURNEY TO THE UNITED
STATES OF AMERICA AND VISIT TO THE
UNITED NATIONS ORGANIZATION
HEADQUARTERS

From the

ADDRESS GIVEN AT THE
CELEBRATION OF VESPERS
AND MEETING WITH THE
BISHOPS OF THE UNITED
STATES OF AMERICA

National Shrine of the Immaculate Conception in
Washington, D.C.
Wednesday, 16 April 2008

Christ, transforming darkness into light

Priests, too, need your guidance and closeness during this
difficult time.[32] They have experienced shame over what has
occurred, and there are those who feel they have lost some of the
trust and esteem they once enjoyed. Not a few are experiencing
a closeness to Christ in his Passion as they struggle to come to

---

32. Pope Benedict XVI was referring to the aftermath of the sexual abuse
of children by members of the Catholic community, especially priests or
religious.

terms with the consequences of the crisis. The bishop, as father, brother and friend of his priests, can help them to draw spiritual fruit from this union with Christ by making them aware of the Lord's consoling presence in the midst of their suffering, and by encouraging them to walk with the Lord along the path of hope (cf. *Spe Salvi*, 39). As Pope John Paul II observed six years ago, 'we must be confident that this time of trial will bring a purification of the entire Catholic community', leading to 'a holier priesthood, a holier episcopate and a holier Church' (*Address to the Cardinals of the United States*, 23 April 2002, 4). There are many signs that, during the intervening period, such purification has indeed been taking place. Christ's abiding presence in the midst of our suffering is gradually transforming our darkness into light: all things are indeed being made new in Christ Jesus our hope.

At this stage a vital part of your task is to strengthen relationships with your clergy, especially in those cases where tension has arisen between priests and their bishops in the wake of the crisis. It is important that you continue to show them your concern, to support them, and to lead by example. In this way you will surely help them to encounter the living God, and point them towards the life-transforming hope of which the Gospel speaks. If you yourselves live in a manner closely configured to Christ, the Good Shepherd, who laid down his life for his sheep, you will inspire your brother priests to rededicate themselves to the service of their flocks with Christ-like generosity. Indeed a clearer focus upon the imitation of Christ in holiness of life is exactly what is needed in order for us to move forward. We need to rediscover the joy of living a Christ-centred life, cultivating the virtues, and immersing ourselves in prayer. When the faithful know that their pastor is a man who prays and who dedicates his life to serving them, they respond with warmth and affection which nourishes and sustains the life of the whole community.

Time spent in prayer is never wasted, however urgent the duties that press upon us from every side. Adoration of Christ our Lord in the Blessed Sacrament prolongs and intensifies the union with him that is established through the Eucharistic celebration (cf. *Sacramentum Caritatis*, 66). Contemplation of the mysteries of the Rosary releases all their saving power and it conforms, unites and consecrates us to Jesus Christ (cf. *Rosarium Virginis Mariae*, 11, 15). Fidelity to the Liturgy of the Hours ensures that the whole of our day is sanctified and it continually reminds us of the need to remain focused on doing God's work, however many pressures and distractions may arise from the task at hand. Thus our devotion helps us to speak and act *in persona Christi*, to teach, govern and sanctify the faithful in the name of Jesus, to bring his reconciliation, his healing and his love to all his beloved brothers and sisters. This radical configuration to Christ, the Good Shepherd, lies at the heart of our pastoral ministry, and if we open ourselves through prayer to the power of the Spirit, he will give us the gifts we need to carry out our daunting task, so that we need never 'be anxious how to speak or what to say' (Mt 10: 19).

APOSTOLIC JOURNEY TO THE UNITED
STATES OF AMERICA AND VISIT TO THE
UNITED NATIONS ORGANIZATION
HEADQUARTERS

From the

RESPONSES GIVEN TO THE QUESTIONS POSED BY THE BISHOPS AT A MEETING WITH THE BISHOPS OF THE UNITED STATES OF AMERICA

*National Shrine of the Immaculate Conception in
Washington, D.C.
Wednesday, 16 April 2008*

Listening together to the voice of the Spirit

Let us be quite frank: the ability to cultivate vocations to the priesthood and the religious life is a sure sign of the health of a local Church. There is no room for complacency in this regard. God continues to call young people; it is up to all of us to encourage a generous and free response to that call. On the other hand, none of us can take this grace for granted.

In the Gospel, Jesus tells us to pray that the Lord of the harvest will send workers. He even admits that the workers are few in comparison with the abundance of the harvest (cf.

Mt 9: 37-38). Strange to say, I often think that prayer – the *unum necessarium*[33] – is the one aspect of vocations work which we tend to forget or to undervalue!

Nor am I speaking only of prayer *for vocations*. Prayer itself, born in Catholic families, nurtured by programs of Christian formation, strengthened by the grace of the sacraments, is the first means by which we come to know the Lord's will for our lives. To the extent that we teach young people to pray, and to pray well, we will be cooperating with God's call. Programs, plans and projects have their place; but the discernment of a vocation is above all the fruit of an intimate dialogue between the Lord and his disciples. Young people, if they know how to pray, can be trusted to know what to do with God's call.

It has been noted that there is a growing thirst for holiness in many young people today, and that, although fewer in number, those who come forward show great idealism and much promise. It is important to listen to them, to understand their experiences, and to encourage them to help their peers to see the need for committed priests and religious, as well as the beauty of a life of sacrificial service to the Lord and his Church. To my mind, much is demanded of vocation directors and formators: candidates today, as much as ever, need to be given a sound intellectual and human formation which will enable them not only to respond to the real questions and needs of their contemporaries, but also to mature in their own conversion and to persevere in life-long commitment to their vocation. As bishops, you are conscious of the sacrifice demanded when you are asked to release one of your finest priests for seminary work. I urge you to respond with generosity, for the good of the whole Church.

Finally, I think you know from experience that most of your brother priests are happy in their vocation. What I said in my

---

33. *The one necessary thing* (Lk 10: 42).

address about the importance of unity and cooperation within the presbyterate applies here too. There is a need for all of us to move beyond sterile divisions, disagreements and preconceptions, and to listen together to the voice of the Spirit who is guiding the Church into a future of hope. Each of us knows how important priestly fraternity has been in our lives. That fraternity is not only a precious possession, but also an immense resource for the renewal of the priesthood and the raising up of new vocations. I would close by encouraging you to foster opportunities for ever greater dialogue and fraternal encounter among your priests, and especially the younger priests. I am convinced that this will bear great fruit for their own enrichment, for the increase of their love for the priesthood and the Church, and for the effectiveness of their apostolate.

Dear Brother Bishops, with these few observations, I once more encourage all of you in your ministry to the faithful entrusted to your pastoral care, and I commend you to the loving intercession of Mary Immaculate, Mother of the Church.

From the

ADDRESS TO PRIESTS, DEACONS AND SEMINARIANS OF THE ARCHDIOCESE OF BRINDISI

Cathedral of Brindisi
Sunday, 15 June 2008

'Through harmony of hearts'

Dear brothers, in seeing you gathered in this church, in which many of you received your diaconal and presbyteral ordination, I remember the words that St Ignatius of Antioch wrote to the Christians of Ephesus: 'Your excellent presbyters, who are a credit to God, are as suited to the Bishop as strings to a harp. So in your harmony of mind and heart the song you sing is Jesus Christ.' And the holy bishop added: 'Every one of you should form a choir, so that, in harmony of sound through harmony of hearts, and in unity taking the note from God, you may sing with one voice through Jesus Christ to the Father. If you do this, he will listen to you' (*Letter to the Ephesians,* 4). Persevere, dear priests, in seeking this unity of intention and reciprocal help, so that fraternal charity and unity in pastoral work are an example and incentive for your communities. This, above all, was the goal of the pastoral visits your Archbishop made to your parishes which ended last March. Due, precisely, to your generous collaboration, it was not merely a juridical exercise but an extraordinary event of ecclesial and formative value. I am certain that it will be fruitful since the Lord will make the seed sown with love grow abundantly in the hearts of the faithful.

I would like to encourage you with my presence today to place yourselves with ever growing openness at the service of the Gospel and of the Church. I know that you already work with zeal and intelligence, sparing no energy in spreading the joyful Gospel proclamation. Christ, to whom you have consecrated your lives, is with you! In him we all believe, to him alone we entrust our lives, it is he whom we desire to proclaim to the world. May Christ who is the Way, the Truth and the Life (cf. Jn 14: 6), be the object of our thought, the topic of our words, the reason for our life. Dear brother priests, if your faith is to be strong and vigorous, as you well know, it must be nourished with assiduous prayer. Thus be models of prayer, become masters of prayer. May your days be marked by times of prayer, during which, after Jesus' example, you engage in a regenerating conversation with the Father. I know it is not easy to stay faithful to this daily appointment with the Lord, especially today when the pace of life is frenetic and worries absorb us more and more. Yet we must convince ourselves: the time he spends in prayer is the most important time in a priest's life, in which divine grace acts with greater effectiveness, making his ministry fruitful. The first service to render to the community is prayer. And therefore, time for prayer must be given a true priority in our life. I know that there are many urgent things: as regards myself, an audience, a document to study, a meeting or something else. But if we are not interiorly in communion with God we cannot even give anything to others. Therefore, God is the first priority. We must always reserve the time necessary to be in communion of prayer with our Lord.

From the

ADDRESS TO THE COMMUNITY OF THE PONTIFICAL ECCLESIASTICAL ACADEMY

Hall of Popes
Monday, 9 June 2008

'Live by faith in the Son of God'

The apostolic and diplomatic ministry at the service of the Holy See that you will carry out wherever you are sent requires skills that cannot be improvised. . . . For this reason, in addition to the necessary and obligatory juridical, theological and diplomatic training, what matters most and marks your life is that your activity reflect a faithful love for Christ and for the Church that inspires in you a welcoming pastoral concern for all.

To carry out this task faithfully, seek from this very moment to 'live by faith in the Son of God' (Gal 2: 20); in other words, strive to be pastors according to the Heart of Christ who engage in daily and intimate conversation with him. Unity with Jesus is the secret of authentic success for every priest's ministry. Whatever work you carry out in the Church, always seek to remain his true friends, faithful friends who have encountered him and have learned to love him above all else. Communion with him, the divine Master of our souls, will guarantee you peace and quiet even in the most complex and difficult moments.

Caught up in the vortex of frenetic activity, humanity often runs the risk of losing the meaning of life, while a certain contemporary culture casts doubt on every absolute value and even on the possibility of recognizing truth and goodness. It is therefore necessary to witness to the presence of God, a God who understands man and can speak to his heart. Your precise task will be to proclaim the joyful and comforting news of the Gospel of love with your way of life even before your words in contexts that are sometimes very distant from the Christian experience. Thus, be docile listeners to the Word of God every day; live in it and live by it so as to make it present in your priestly activity. Proclaim the truth that is Christ. May prayer, meditation and listening to the Word of God be your daily bread. If communion with Jesus grows within you, if you live by him and not only for him, you will radiate his love and glory around you.

Besides listening daily to the Word of God, may the celebration of the Eucharist be the heart and centre of every one of your days and of your entire ministry. Priests, like every baptized person, live by Eucharistic communion with the Lord. It is impossible to receive the Lord every day, taking his Body and Blood into our hands, pronouncing the tremendous and wonderful words: 'This is my Body, this is my Blood' without letting ourselves be seized by him, without letting ourselves be won over by fascination for him, without letting his infinite love change us from within. May the Eucharist become a school of life for you in which Jesus' sacrifice on the Cross teaches you to make a total gift of yourselves to your brethren.

APOSTOLIC JOURNEY OF HIS HOLINESS BENEDICT XVI TO SYDNEY (AUSTRALIA) ON THE OCCASION OF THE 23rd WORLD YOUTH DAY (12-21 JULY, 2008)

From the

INTERVIEW GIVEN DURING THE FLIGHT TO AUSTRALIA

Saturday, 12 July 2008

'In the service of Our Lord'

Speaking of the crisis caused by sexual abuse Pope Benedict said:

The problem is essentially the same as in the United States. I felt obliged to speak about it in the United States because it is essential for the Church to reconcile, to prevent, to help and also to see guilt in these problems, so I will essentially say the same things as I said in America. As I said we have three dimensions to clarify: the first I mention is our moral teaching. It must be clear, it was always clear from the first centuries that priesthood, to be a priest, is incompatible with this behaviour, because the priest is in the service of Our Lord, and Our Lord is holiness in person, and always teaching us – the Church has always insisted on this. We have to reflect on what was insufficient in our education, in our teaching in recent decades: there was, in the 50s, 60s and 70s, the idea of proportionalism in ethics: it held that no thing is bad in itself, but only in proportion to others; with proportionalism it was possible to think for some subjects – one could also be paedophilia – that in some proportion they could be a good thing. Now, it must be stated clearly, this was never Catholic doctrine. There are things which are always bad, and paedophilia is always bad. In our education, in the seminaries, in our permanent formation of the priests, we have to help priests to really be close to Christ, to learn from Christ, and so to be helpers, and not adversaries of our fellow human beings, of our Christians. So, we will do everything possible to clarify what is the teaching of the Church and help in the education and in the preparation of priests, in permanent formation, and we will do all possible to heal and to reconcile the victims. I think this is the essential content of what the word 'apologize' says. I think it is better, more important to give the content of the formula, and I think the content has to say what was insufficient in our behaviour, what we must do in this moment, how we can prevent and how we all can heal and reconcile.

From the

MEETING WITH THE CLERGY OF THE DIOCESE OF BOLZANO-BRESSANONE

Cathedral of Brixen
Wednesday, 6 August 2008

Fr Franz Pixner, dean at Kastelruth: *Holy Father, I am Franz Pixner and I am the pastor of two large parishes. I myself, together with many of my confreres and lay persons, are concerned about the increasing burden of pastoral care caused by, for example, the pastoral units that are being created: the intense pressure of work, the lack of recognition, difficulties concerning the Magisterium, loneliness, the dwindling number of priests but also of communities of the faithful. Many people wonder what God is asking of us in this situation and how the Holy Spirit wishes to encourage us. In this context arise questions concerning, for example, the celibacy of priests, the ordination of* viri probati[34] *to the priesthood, the involvement of charisms, particularly those of women, in pastoral care, making men and women collaborators trained in theology responsible for conferring Baptism and preaching homilies. The question is also asked how we priests, confronted by the new challenges, can help one another in a brotherly community, at the various*

---

34. *Tested men.* The phrase *viri probati* is most commonly used with regards the question of ordaining married men.

levels of the diocese, diaconate and pastoral and parish unit. We ask you, Holy Father, to give us some good advice for all these questions. Thank you!

Pope Benedict XVI: Dear dean, you have opened a whole series of questions that occupy and concern pastors and all of us in this age, and you certainly know that I cannot answer all of them here. I imagine that you will have repeated opportunities to consider them with your bishop and we in turn we will speak of them at the Synod of Bishops. All of us, I believe, stand in need of this dialogue with one another, of the dialogue of faith and responsibility, in order to find the straight narrow path in this era, full of difficult perspectives on faith and challenges for priests. No one has an instant recipe, we are all searching together.

With this reservation, I find myself together with all of you in the midst of this process of toil and interior struggle, I shall try to say a few words, precisely as part of a broader dialogue.

In my answer I would like to examine two fundamental aspects: on the one hand, the irreplaceableness of the priest, the meaning and the manner of the priestly ministry today; and on the other – and this is more obvious than it used to be – the multiplicity of charisms and the fact that all together they are Church, they build the Church and for this reason we must strive to reawaken charisms. We must foster this lively whole which in turn then also supports the priest. He supports others, others support him and only in this complex and variegated whole can the Church develop today and toward the future.

On the one hand, there will always be a need for the priest who is totally dedicated to the Lord and therefore totally dedicated to humanity. In the Old Testament there is the call to 'sanctification' which more or less corresponds to what we mean today by 'consecration', or even 'priestly Ordination': something is delivered over to God and is therefore removed from the common sphere, it is given to him. Yet this means that it is now available for all. Since it has been taken and given to God, for this very reason it is now not isolated by being raised from the 'for', to the 'for all'. I think that this can also be said of the Church's priesthood. It means on the one hand that we are consigned to the Lord, separated from ordinary life, but on the other, we are consigned to him because in this way we can belong to him totally and totally belong to others. I believe we must continuously seek to show this to young people – to those who are idealists, who want to do something for the whole – show them that precisely this 'extraction from the common' means 'consignment to the whole' and that this is an important way, the most important way, to serve our brethren. Part of this, moreover, is truly making oneself available to the Lord in the fullness of one's being and consequently, finding oneself totally available to men and women. I think celibacy is a fundamental expression of this totality and already, for this reason, an important reference in this world because it only has meaning if we truly believe in eternal life and if we believe that God involves us and that we can be for him.

Therefore, the priesthood is indispensable because in the Eucharist itself, originating in God, the Church is built; in the Sacrament of Penance purification is conferred; in the Sacrament, the priesthood is, precisely, an involvement in the 'for' of Jesus Christ. However, I know well how difficult it is today – when a priest finds himself directing not only one easily managed parish but several parishes and pastoral units; when he must be available to give this or that advice, and so forth – how difficult it is to live such a life. I believe that in this situation it is important to have the courage to limit oneself and to be clear about deciding on priorities. A fundamental priority of priestly life is to be with the Lord and thus to have time for prayer. St Charles Borromeo always used to say: 'You will not be able to care for the souls of others if you let your own perish. In the end you will no longer do anything even for others. You must always have time for being with God.' I would therefore like to emphasize: whatever the demands that arise, it is a real priority to find every day, I would say, an hour to be in silence for the Lord and with the Lord, as the Church suggests we do with the breviary, with daily prayers, so as to continually enrich ourselves inwardly, to return – as I said in answering the first question – to within the reach of the Holy Spirit's breath. And to order priorities on this basis: I must learn to see what is truly essential, where my presence as a priest is indispensable and where I cannot delegate to anyone else. And at the same time, I must humbly accept when there are many things I should do and where my presence is requested that I cannot manage because I know my limits. I think people understand this humility.

And I now must link the other aspect to this: knowing how to delegate, to get people to collaborate. I have the impression that people understand and also appreciate it when a priest is with God, when he is concerned with his office of being the person who prays for others: 'we', they say, 'cannot pray so much, you must do it for us: basically, it is your job, as it were, to be the one who prays for us.' They want a priest who honestly endeavours to live with the Lord and then is available to men and women – the suffering, the dying, the sick, children, young people (I would say that they are the priorities) – but also who can distinguish between things that others do better than him, thereby making room for those gifts. I am thinking of Movements and of many other forms of collaboration in the parish. May all these things also be reflected upon in the diocese itself, new forms of collaboration should be created and interchanges encouraged. You rightly said that in this it is important to look beyond the parish to the diocesan community, indeed, to the community of the universal Church which in her turn must direct her gaze to see what is happening in the parish and what the consequences are for the individual priest.

You then touched on another point, very important in my eyes: priests, even if they live far apart are a true community of brothers who should support and help one another. In order not to drift into isolation, into loneliness with its sorrows, it is important for us to meet one another regularly. It will be the task of the diocese to establish how best to organize meetings for priests – today we have cars which make travelling easier – so that we can experience being together ever anew, learn from one another, mutually correct and help one another, cheer one another and comfort one another, so that in this communion of the presbyterate, together with the bishop we can carry out our service to the local Church. Precisely: no priest is a priest on his own; we are a presbyterate and it is only in this communion with the bishop that each one can carry out his service. Now, this beautiful communion recognized by all at the theological level, must also be expressed in practice in the ways identified by the local Church, and it must be extended because no bishop is a bishop on his own but only a bishop in the College, in the great communion of bishops. This is the communion we should always strive for. And I think that it is a particularly beautiful aspect of Catholicism: through the Primacy, which is not an absolute monarchy but a service of communion, that we may have the certainty of this unity. Thus in a large community with many voices, all together we make the great music of faith ring out in this world.

Let us pray the Lord to comfort us when we think we cannot manage any longer: let us support one another and then the Lord will help us to find the right paths together.

Fr Paolo Rizzi, parish priest and lecturer in theology at the Higher Institute for Religious Sciences: *Holy Father, I am parish priest and lecturer in theology at the Higher Institute for Religious Sciences. We would like to hear your pastoral opinion about the situation concerning the Sacraments of First Communion and Confirmation. Always more often the children, boys and girls, who receive these Sacraments prepare themselves with commitment to the catechetical meetings but do not take part in the Sunday Eucharist, and then one wonders: what is the point of all this? At times we might feel like saying: 'Then just stay at home.' Instead we continue as always to accept them, believing that in any case it is better not to extinguish the wick of the little flickering flame. We think, that is, that in any case, the gift of the Spirit can have an effect beyond what we can see, and that in an epoch of transition like this one it is more prudent not to make drastic decisions. More generally, 35 years ago I thought that we were beginning to be a little flock, a minority community, more or less everywhere in Europe; that we should therefore administer the sacraments only to those who are truly committed to Christian life. Then, partly because of the style of John Paul II's Pontificate, I thought things through again. If it is possible to make predictions for the future, what do you think? What pastoral approaches can you suggest to us? Thank you.*

Pope Benedict XVI: Well, I cannot give an infallible answer here, I can only seek to respond according to what I see. I must say that I took a similar route to yours. When I was younger I was rather severe. I said: the sacraments are sacraments of faith, and where faith does not exist, where the practice of faith does not exist, the Sacrament cannot be conferred either. And then I always used to talk to my parish priests when I was Archbishop of Munich: here too there were two factions, one severe and one broad-minded. Then I too, with time, came to realize that we must follow, rather, the example of the Lord, who was very open even with people on the margins of Israel of that time. He was a Lord of mercy, too open – according to many official authorities – with sinners, welcoming them or letting them invite him to their dinners, drawing them to him in his communion.

Therefore I would say substantially that the sacraments are naturally sacraments of faith: when there is no element of faith, when First Communion is no more than a great lunch with beautiful clothes and beautiful gifts, it can no longer be a sacrament of faith. Yet, on the other hand, if we can still see a little flame of desire for Communion in the faith, a desire even in these children who want to enter into communion with Jesus, it seems to me that it is right to be rather broad-minded. Naturally, of course, one purpose of our catechesis must be to make children understand that Communion, First Communion, is not a 'fixed' event, but requires a continuity of friendship with Jesus, a journey with Jesus. I know that children often have the intention and desire to go to Sunday Mass but their parents do not make this desire possible. If we see that children want it, that they have the desire to go, this seems to me almost a sacrament of desire, the 'will' to participate in Sunday Mass. In this sense, we naturally must do our best in the context of preparation for the sacraments to reach the parents as well, and thus to – let us say – awaken in them too a sensitivity to the process in which their child is involved. They should help their children to follow their own desire to enter into friendship with Jesus, which is a form of life, of the future. If parents want their children to be able to make their First Communion, this somewhat social desire must be extended into a religious one, to make a journey with Jesus possible.

I would say, therefore, that in the context of the catechesis of children, that work with parents is very important. And this is precisely one of the opportunities to meet with parents, making the life of faith also present to the adults, because, it seems to me, they themselves can relearn the faith from the children and understand that this great solemnity is only meaningful, true and authentic if it is celebrated in the context of a journey with

Jesus, in the context of a life of faith. Thus, one should endeavour to convince parents, through their children, of the need for a preparatory journey that is expressed in participation in the mysteries and that begins to make these mysteries loved. I would say that this is definitely an inadequate answer, but the pedagogy of faith is always a journey and we must accept today's situations. Yet, we must also open them more to each person, so that the result is not only an external memory of things that endures but that their hearts have truly been touched. The moment when we are convinced the heart is touched – it has felt a little of Jesus' love, it has felt a little the desire to move along these lines and in this direction. That is the moment when, it seems to me, we can say that we have made a true catechesis. The proper meaning of catechesis, in fact, must be this: to bring the flame of Jesus' love, even if it is a small one, to the hearts of children, and through the children to their parents, thus reopening the places of faith in our time.

PASTORAL VISIT TO
CAGLIARI – SARDINIA

From the

ADDRESS GIVEN AT THE MEETING WITH PRIESTS, SEMINARIANS AND STUDENTS OF THE PONTIFICAL THEOLOGICAL FACULTY OF SARDINIA

Cathedral of Cagliari
Sunday, 7 September 2008

'God wants you for himself'

Now I affectionately address the community of seminarians and of the Theological Faculty, where many of you have been able to carry out doctrinal and pastoral formation, and where currently many young people go to prepare for their future ministerial priesthood. I am anxious to thank the teachers and professors who dedicate themselves daily to such an important apostolic work. To accompany candidates for the priestly mission on their formative journey means above all to help them conform themselves to Christ. In this duty, you, dear educators and professors, are called to play an irreplaceable role, since it is truly during these years that one lays the foundations of their future priestly ministry. This is why, as on different occasions I have been able to emphasize, it is necessary to guide seminarians to a personal experience of God through personal and communal daily prayer, and above all through the Eucharist, celebrated and experienced as the centre of their very existence. In the Post-Synodal Exhortation *Pastores Dabo Vobis* John Paul II wrote: 'Intellectual formation in theology and formation in the spiritual life, in particular the life of prayer, meet and strengthen each other, without detracting in any way from the soundness of research or from the spiritual tenor of prayer' (n. 53).

Dear seminarians and students of the Theological Faculty, you know that theological formation – as my Venerable Predecessor recalled further in the cited Apostolic Exhortation – is very complex and demanding work. It must lead you to possess a 'complete and unified' vision of revealed truths and of their acceptance into the faith experience of the Church. From this pours forth the double demand of knowing the entirety of Christian truth and knowing those truths not as truths separated one from the other, but in an organic way, as a union, as the one truth of faith in God, building 'a synthesis which will be the result of the contributions of the different theological disciplines, the specific nature of which acquires genuine value only in their profound coordination' (ibid., n. 54). This [synthesis] demonstrates to us the unity of truth, the unity of our faith. Besides, in these years, each activity and initiative must dispose you to administer the charity of Christ the Good Shepherd. To him you are called to be tomorrow's ministers and witnesses: ministers of his grace and witnesses of his love. Next to study and pastoral and apostolic experience from which you can draw, do not forget, however, to put the constant quest for intimate communion with Christ in the first place. Here, only here, rests the secret of your true apostolic success.

Dear priests, dear aspirants to the priesthood and to consecrated life, God wants you for himself and calls you to be workers in his vineyard, just as he did many men and women throughout the Christian history of your beautiful island. They knew to respond with a generous 'yes' to his call. I am thinking of, for example, the evangelizing work carried out by the religious: from the Franciscans to the Mercedarians, from the Dominicans to the Jesuits, from the Benedictines to the Vincentians, from the Salesians to the Piarists, from the Christian Brothers to the Josephine Fathers, to the Sons of Divine Providence and so many others still. And how could the great flowering of female religious vocations, for which Sardinia has been a true and proper garden, be forgotten? In many Orders and Congregations Sardinian women are present, especially in cloistered monasteries. Without this great 'cloud of witnesses' (cf. Heb 12: 1) it certainly would have been much more difficult to spread the love of Christ in the towns, families, schools, hospitals, prisons and workplaces. What a heritage of good has come, accumulating grace by their dedication! Without the seed of Christianity Sardinia would be more fragile and poor. Together with you I thank God who never lets the witnesses of saints fail to guide his people!

Dear brothers and sisters, it is now up to you to carry on the work of good accomplished by those who have gone before you. To you, in particular, dear priests – and I address with affection all the priests of Sardinia – I assure my spiritual nearness, so that you may respond to the Lord's call with total loyalty as, even recently, some of your brothers have done. I recall Fr Graziano Muntoni, a priest of the Diocese of Nuoro, killed on Christmas Eve of 1998, while he was going to celebrate Mass, and Fr Battore Carzedda of the P.I.M.E., who gave his life so that believers of all religions would open to sincere dialogue sustained by love. Do not be frightened, do not be discouraged by difficulties: the grain and the weeds, as we know, will grow together until the end of the world (cf. Mt 13: 30). It is important to be seeds of good grain which, fallen to earth, bear fruit. Deepen the awareness of your identity: the priest, for the Church and in the Church, is a humble but real sign of the one, eternal Priest who is Jesus. He must proclaim his word authoritatively, renew his acts of pardon and offering and exercise loving concern in the service of his flock, in communion with the pastors and faithfully docile to the teaching of the Magisterium. Therefore, rekindle the charism you have received with the imposition of hands (cf. II Tm 1: 6) each day, identifying with Jesus Christ in his triple function of sanctifying, teaching and shepherding the flock. May Mary Most Holy, Mother of the Church, protect you and accompany you. On my behalf I bless all of you, with a special remembrance for the elderly and sick priests, and for all the people entrusted to your pastoral care.

Thank you for this meeting and best wishes for your ministry.

APOSTOLIC JOURNEY OF HIS HOLINESS BENEDICT XVI TO FRANCE ON THE OCCASION OF THE 150th ANNIVERSARY OF THE APPARITIONS OF THE BLESSED VIRGIN MARY AT LOURDES (12-15 SEPTEMBER, 2008)

From the

ADDRESS GIVEN TO THE FRENCH EPISCOPAL CONFERENCE

Conference Hall of Saint Bernadette's Church, Lourdes
Sunday, 14 September 2008

'Preach the word, be urgent in season and out of season . . . be unfailing in patience and in teaching' (II Tim 4: 2)

In order to accomplish this task effectively, you need co-workers. For this reason, priestly and religious vocations deserve to be encouraged more than ever. I have been informed of the initiatives that have been taken with faith in this area, and I hasten to offer my full support to those who are not afraid, as Christ was not afraid, to invite the young and not so young to place themselves at the service of the Master who is here, calling (cf. Mt 11: 28). I would like to offer warm thanks and encouragement to all families, parishes, Christian communities and ecclesial movements, which provide the fertile soil that bears the good fruit (cf. Mt 13: 8) of vocations. In this context, I wish to acknowledge the countless prayers of true disciples of Christ and of his Church. These include priests, men and women religious, the elderly, the sick, as well as prisoners, who for decades have offered prayers to God in obedience to the command of Jesus: 'Pray therefore the Lord of the harvest to send out labourers into his harvest' (Mt 9: 38). The bishop and the communities of the faithful must play their part in promoting and welcoming priestly and religious vocations, relying on the grace of the Holy Spirit in order to carry out the necessary discernment. Yes, dear Brothers in the episcopate, continue inviting people to the priesthood and the religious life, just as Peter let down the nets at the Master's order, when he had spent the whole night fishing without catching anything (cf. Lk 5: 5).

It can never be said often enough that the priesthood is indispensable to the Church, for it is at the service of the laity. Priests are a gift from God for the Church. Where their specific missions are concerned, priests cannot delegate their functions to the faithful. Dear Brothers in the episcopate, I urge you to continue helping your priests to live in profound union with Christ. Their spiritual life is the foundation of their apostolic life. You will gently exhort them to daily prayer and to the worthy celebration of the sacraments, especially the Eucharist and Reconciliation, as Saint Francis de Sales did for his priests. Every priest should be able to feel happiness in serving the Church. In the school of the Curé d'Ars, a son of your land and patron of pastors throughout the world, constantly reiterate that the greatest thing a man can do is to give the body and blood of Christ to the faithful and to forgive their sins. Seek to be attentive to their human, intellectual and spiritual formation, and to their means of subsistence. Try, despite the weight of your onerous tasks, to meet them regularly and know how to receive them as brothers and friends (cf. *Lumen Gentium*, 28; *Christus Dominus*,

16). Priests need your affection, your encouragement and your solicitude. Be close to them and have particular care for those who are in difficulties, sick or elderly (cf. *Christus Dominus*, 16). Do not forget that they are – as the Second Vatican Council teaches, quoting the magnificent expression used by Saint Ignatius of Antioch in his Letter to the Magnesians – 'the spiritual crown of the Bishop' (*Lumen Gentium*, 41).

Liturgical worship is the supreme expression of priestly and episcopal life, just as it is of catechetical teaching. Your duty to sanctify the faithful people, dear Brothers, is indispensable for the growth of the Church. In the *Motu Proprio 'Summorum Pontificum'*, I was led to set out the conditions in which this duty is to be exercised, with regard to the possibility of using the missal of Blessed John XXIII (1962) in addition to that of Pope Paul VI (1970). Some fruits of these new arrangements have already been seen, and I hope that, thanks be to God, the necessary pacification of spirits is already taking place. I am aware of your difficulties, but I do not doubt that, within a reasonable time, you can find solutions satisfactory for all, lest the seamless tunic of Christ be further torn. Everyone has a place in the Church. Every person, without exception, should be able to feel at home, and never rejected. God, who loves all men and women and wishes none to be lost, entrusts us with this mission by appointing us shepherds of his sheep. We can only thank him for the honour and the trust that he has placed in us. Let us therefore strive always to be servants of unity!

III.

SACRAMENTUM CARITATIS

III

In persona Christi capitis

SACRAMENTUM CARITATIS

23. The intrinsic relationship between the Eucharist and the sacrament of Holy Orders clearly emerges from Jesus' own words in the Upper Room: "Do this in memory of me" (Lk 22: 19). On the night before he died, Jesus instituted the Eucharist and at the same time established the priesthood of the New Covenant. He is priest, victim and altar: the mediator between God the Father and his people (cf. Heb 5: 5-10), the victim of atonement (cf. 1 Jn 2: 2, 4, 10) who offers himself on the altar of the Cross. No one can say: this is my body and this is the cup of my blood, except in the name and in the person of Christ, the one high priest of the new and eternal Covenant.

35. This Apostolic Exhortation was Pope Benedict XVI's response to the Eleventh Ordinary General Assembly of the Synod of Bishops held in the Vatican from 2–23 October 2005. Pope John Paul II had declared 2005 to be the Year of the Eucharist and asked the Synod Fathers to reflect on this sacrament. In this chapter those paragraphs which particularly address the relationship between the Eucharist and the priesthood have been selected, retaining the original numbering of paragraphs, and audience provided at the end of the chapter as in the original document to facilitate cross referencing to the complete document.

From the

APOSTOLIC EXHORTATION SACRAMENTUM CARITATIS

22 February 2007[35]

The Eucharist and the Sacrament of Holy Orders

In persona Christi capitis

23. The intrinsic relationship between the Eucharist and the sacrament of Holy Orders clearly emerges from Jesus' own words in the Upper Room: 'Do this in memory of me' (Lk 22: 19). On the night before he died, Jesus instituted the Eucharist and at the same time established the *priesthood of the New Covenant*. He is priest, victim and altar: the mediator between God the Father and his people (cf. Heb 5: 5-10), the victim of atonement (cf. I Jn 2: 2, 4: 10) who offers himself on the altar of the Cross. No one can say 'this is my body' and 'this is the cup of my blood' except in the name and in the person of Christ, the one high priest of the new and eternal Covenant

---

35. This Apostolic Exhortation was Pope Benedict XVI's response to the Eleventh Ordinary General Assembly of the Synod of Bishops held in the Vatican from 2 – 23 October 2005. Pope John Paul II had declared 2005 to be the Year of the Eucharist and asked the Synod Fathers to reflect on this Sacrament. In this chapter those paragraphs which particularly address the relationship between the Eucharist and the priesthood have been selected, retaining the original numbering of paragraphs and endnotes (provided at the end of the chapter) as in the original document to facilitate cross referencing to the complete document.

(cf. Heb 8-9). Earlier meetings of the Synod of Bishops had considered the question of the ordained priesthood, both with regard to the nature of the ministry (69) and the formation of candidates. (70) Here, in the light of the discussion that took place during the last Synod, I consider it important to recall several important points about the relationship between the sacrament of the Eucharist and Holy Orders. First of all, we need to stress once again that the connection between *Holy Orders and the Eucharist* is seen most clearly at Mass, when the bishop or priest presides *in the person of Christ the Head.*

The Church teaches that priestly ordination is the indispensable condition for the valid celebration of the Eucharist. (71) Indeed, 'in the ecclesial service of the ordained minister, it is Christ himself who is present to his Church as Head of his Body, Shepherd of his flock, High Priest of the redemptive sacrifice.' (72) Certainly the ordained minister also acts 'in the name of the whole Church, when presenting to God the prayer of the Church, and above all when offering the eucharistic sacrifice.' (73) As a result, priests should be conscious of the fact that in their ministry they must never put themselves or their personal opinions in first place, but Jesus Christ. Any attempt to make themselves the centre of the liturgical action contradicts their very identity as priests. The priest is above all a servant of others, and he must continually work at being a sign pointing to Christ, a docile instrument in the Lord's hands. This is seen particularly in his humility in leading the liturgical assembly, in obedience to the rite, uniting himself to it in mind and heart, and avoiding anything that might give the impression of an inordinate emphasis on his own personality. I encourage the clergy always to see their eucharistic ministry as a humble service offered to Christ and his Church. The priesthood, as Saint Augustine said, is *amoris officium,* (74) it is the office of the good shepherd, who offers his life for his sheep (cf. Jn 10: 14-15).

The Eucharist and priestly celibacy

24. The Synod Fathers wished to emphasize that the ministerial priesthood, through ordination, calls for complete configuration to Christ. While respecting the different practice and tradition of the Eastern Churches, there is a need to reaffirm the profound meaning of priestly celibacy, which is rightly considered a priceless treasure, and is also confirmed by the Eastern practice of choosing bishops only from the ranks of the celibate. These Churches also greatly esteem the decision of many priests to embrace celibacy. This choice on the part of the priest expresses in a special way the dedication which conforms him to Christ and his exclusive offering of himself for the Kingdom of God. (75) The fact that Christ himself, the eternal priest, lived his mission even to the sacrifice of the Cross in the state of virginity constitutes the sure point of reference for understanding the meaning of the tradition of the Latin Church. It is not sufficient to understand priestly celibacy in purely functional terms. Celibacy is really a special way of conforming oneself to Christ's own way of life. This choice has first and foremost a nuptial meaning; it is a profound identification with the heart of Christ the Bridegroom who gives his life for his Bride. In continuity with the great ecclesial tradition, with the Second Vatican Council (76) and with my predecessors in the papacy, (77) I reaffirm the beauty and the importance of a priestly life lived in celibacy as a sign expressing total and exclusive devotion to Christ, to the Church and to the Kingdom of God, and I therefore confirm that it remains obligatory in the Latin tradition. Priestly celibacy lived with maturity, joy and dedication is an immense blessing for the Church and for society itself.

The clergy shortage and the pastoral care of vocations

25. In the light of the connection between the sacrament of Holy Orders and the Eucharist, the Synod considered the

difficult situation that has arisen in various dioceses which face a shortage of priests. This happens not only in some areas of first evangelization, but also in many countries of long-standing Christian tradition. Certainly a more equitable distribution of clergy would help to solve the problem. Efforts need to be made to encourage a greater awareness of this situation at every level. Bishops should involve Institutes of Consecrated Life and the new ecclesial groups in their pastoral needs, while respecting their particular charisms, and they should invite the clergy to become more open to serving the Church wherever there is need, even if this calls for sacrifice. (78) The Synod also discussed pastoral initiatives aimed at promoting, especially among the young, an attitude of interior openness to a priestly calling. The situation cannot be resolved by purely practical decisions. On no account should bishops react to real and understandable concerns about the shortage of priests by failing to carry out adequate vocational discernment, or by admitting to seminary formation and ordination candidates who lack the necessary qualities for priestly ministry (79). An insufficiently formed clergy, admitted to ordination without the necessary discernment, will not easily be able to offer a witness capable of evoking in others the desire to respond generously to Christ's call. The pastoral care of vocations needs to involve the entire Christian community in every area of its life. (80) Obviously, this pastoral work on all levels also includes exploring the matter with families, which are often indifferent or even opposed to the idea of a priestly vocation. Families should generously embrace the gift of life and bring up their children to be open to doing God's will. In a word, they must have the courage to set before young people the radical decision to follow Christ, showing them how deeply rewarding it is.

Gratitude and hope

26. Finally, we need to have ever greater faith and hope in God's providence. Even if there is a shortage of priests in some areas, we must never lose confidence that Christ continues to inspire men to leave everything behind and to dedicate themselves totally to celebrating the sacred mysteries, preaching the Gospel and ministering to the flock. In this regard, I wish to express the gratitude of the whole Church for all those bishops and priests who carry out their respective missions with fidelity, devotion and zeal. Naturally, the Church's gratitude also goes to deacons, who receive the laying on of hands 'not for priesthood but for service.' (81) As the Synod Assembly recommended, I offer a special word of thanks to those *fidei donum* priests who work faithfully and generously at building up the community by proclaiming the word of God and breaking the Bread of Life, devoting all their energy to serving the mission of the Church. (82) Let us thank God for all those priests who have suffered even to the sacrifice of their lives in order to serve Christ. The eloquence of their example shows what it means to be a priest to the end. Theirs is a moving witness that can inspire many young people to follow Christ and to expend their lives for others, and thus to discover true life.

Ars celebrandi

38. In the course of the Synod, there was frequent insistence on the need to avoid any antithesis between the *ars celebrandi*, the art of proper celebration, and the full, active and fruitful participation of all the faithful. The primary way to foster the participation of the People of God in the sacred rite is the proper celebration of the rite itself. The *ars celebrandi* is the best way to ensure their *actuosa participatio*. (114) The *ars celebrandi* is the fruit of faithful adherence to the liturgical norms in all their richness; indeed, for two thousand years this

way of celebrating has sustained the faith life of all believers, called to take part in the celebration as the People of God, a royal priesthood, a holy nation (cf. I Pet 2: 4-5, 9).(115)

The Bishop, celebrant par excellence

39. While it is true that the whole People of God participates in the eucharistic liturgy, a correct *ars celebrandi* necessarily entails a specific responsibility on the part of those who have received the sacrament of Holy Orders. Bishops, priests, and deacons, each according to his proper rank, must consider the celebration of the liturgy as their principal duty. (116) Above all, this is true of the Diocesan Bishop: as 'the chief steward of the mysteries of God in the particular Church entrusted to his care, he is the moderator, promoter, and guardian of the whole of its liturgical life.' (117) This is essential for the life of the particular Church, not only because communion with the bishop is required for the lawfulness of every celebration within his territory, but also because he himself is the celebrant par excellence within his diocese. (118) It is his responsibility to ensure unity and harmony in the celebrations taking place in his territory. Consequently the bishop must be 'determined that the priests, the deacons, and the lay Christian faithful grasp ever more deeply the genuine meaning of the rites and liturgical texts, and thereby be led to an active and fruitful celebration of the Eucharist.' (119) I would ask that every effort be made to ensure that the liturgies which the bishop celebrates in his cathedral are carried out with complete respect for the *ars celebrandi,* so that they can be considered an example for the entire diocese. (120)

Respect for the liturgical books and the richness of signs

40. Emphasizing the importance of the *ars celebrandi* also leads to an appreciation of the value of the liturgical norms. (121)

The *ars celebrandi* should foster a sense of the sacred and the use of outward signs which help to cultivate this sense, such as, for example, the harmony of the rite, the liturgical vestments, the furnishings and the sacred space. The eucharistic celebration is enhanced when priests and liturgical leaders are committed to making known the current liturgical texts and norms, making available the great riches found in the *General Instruction of the Roman Missal* and the *Order of Readings for Mass*. Perhaps we take it for granted that our ecclesial communities already know and appreciate these resources, but this is not always the case. These texts contain riches which have preserved and expressed the faith and experience of the People of God over its two-thousand-year history. Equally important for a correct *ars celebrandi* is an attentiveness to the various kinds of language that the liturgy employs: words and music, gestures and silence, movement, the liturgical colours of the vestments. By its very nature the liturgy operates on different levels of communication which enable it to engage the whole human person. The simplicity of its gestures and the sobriety of its orderly sequence of signs communicate and inspire more than any contrived and inappropriate additions. Attentiveness and fidelity to the specific structure of the rite express both a recognition of the nature of Eucharist as a gift and, on the part of the minister, a docile openness to receiving this ineffable gift.

The homily

46. Given the importance of the word of God, the quality of homilies needs to be improved. The homily is 'part of the liturgical action,' (139) and is meant to foster a deeper understanding of the word of God, so that it can bear fruit in the lives of the faithful. Hence ordained ministers must 'prepare the homily carefully, based on an adequate knowledge

of Sacred Scripture.' (140) Generic and abstract homilies should be avoided. In particular, I ask these ministers to preach in such a way that the homily closely relates the proclamation of the word of God to the sacramental celebration (141) and the life of the community, so that the word of God truly becomes the Church's vital nourishment and support. (142) The catechetical and paraenetic aim of the homily should not be forgotten. During the course of the liturgical year it is appropriate to offer the faithful, prudently and on the basis of the three-year lectionary, 'thematic' homilies treating the great themes of the Christian faith, on the basis of what has been authoritatively proposed by the Magisterium in the four 'pillars' of the Catechism of the Catholic Church and the recent Compendium, namely: the profession of faith, the celebration of the Christian mystery, life in Christ and Christian prayer. (143)

Participation and the priestly ministry

53. The beauty and the harmony of the liturgy find eloquent expression in the order by which everyone is called to participate actively. This entails an acknowledgment of the distinct hierarchical roles involved in the celebration. It is helpful to recall that active participation is not per se equivalent to the exercise of a specific ministry. The active participation of the laity does not benefit from the confusion arising from an inability to distinguish, within the Church's communion, the different functions proper to each one. (158) There is a particular need for clarity with regard to the specific functions of the priest. He alone, and no other, as the tradition of the Church attests, presides over the entire eucharistic celebration, from the initial greeting to the final blessing. In virtue of his reception of Holy Orders, he represents Jesus Christ, the head of the Church, and, in a specific way, also the Church

herself. (159) Every celebration of the Eucharist, in fact, is led by the bishop, 'either in person or through priests who are his helpers.' (160) He is helped by a deacon, who has specific duties during the celebration: he prepares the altar, assists the priest, proclaims the Gospel, preaches the homily from time to time, reads the intentions of the Prayer of the Faithful, and distributes the Eucharist to the faithful. (161) Associated with these ministries linked to the sacrament of Holy Orders, there are also other ministries of liturgical service which can be carried out in a praiseworthy manner by religious and properly trained laity. (162)

The Eucharist and priestly spirituality

80. The eucharistic form of the Christian life is seen in a very special way in the priesthood. Priestly spirituality is intrinsically eucharistic. The seeds of this spirituality are already found in the words spoken by the bishop during the ordination liturgy: 'Receive the oblation of the holy people to be offered to God. Understand what you do, imitate what you celebrate, and conform your life to the mystery of the Lord's Cross.' (222) In order to give an ever greater eucharistic form to his existence, the priest, beginning with his years in the seminary, should make his spiritual life his highest priority. (223) He is called to seek God tirelessly, while remaining attuned to the concerns of his brothers and sisters. An intense spiritual life will enable him to enter more deeply into communion with the Lord and to let himself be possessed by God's love, bearing witness to that love at all times, even the darkest and most difficult. To this end I join the Synod Fathers in recommending 'the daily celebration of Mass, even when the faithful are not present.' (224) This recommendation is consistent with the objectively infinite value of every celebration of the Eucharist, and is motivated by the Mass's unique spiritual fruitfulness. If celebrated in a faith-

filled and attentive way, Mass is formative in the deepest sense of the word, since it fosters the priest's configuration to Christ and strengthens him in his vocation.

Endnotes

(69) Cf. Synod of Bishops, Second General Assembly, Document on the Ministerial Priesthood *Ultimis Temporibus* (30 November 1971): AAS 63 (1971), 898-942.

(70) Cf. John Paul II, Post-Synodal Apostolic Exhortation *Pastores Dabo Vobis* (25 March 1992), 42-69: AAS 84 (1992), 729-778.

(71) Cf. Second Vatican Ecumenical Council, Dogmatic Constitution on the Church *Lumen Gentium*, 10; Congregation for the Doctrine of the Faith, Letter on Certain Questions Concerning the Minister of the Eucharist *Sacerdotium Ministeriale* (6 August 1983): AAS 75 (1983), 1001-1009.

(72) *Catechism of the Catholic Church*, 1548.

(73) Ibid., 1552.

(74) Cf. *In Iohannis Evangelium Tractatus*, 123, 5: PL 35, 1967.

(75) Cf. *Propositio* 11.

(76) Cf. Decree on the Ministry and Life of Priests *Presbyterorum Ordinis*, 16.

(77) Cf. John XXIII, Encyclical Letter *Sacerdotii Nostri Primordia* (1 August 1959): AAS 51 (1959), 545-579; Paul VI, Encyclical Letter *Sacerdotalis Coelibatus* (24 June 1967): AAS 59 (1967), 657-697; John Paul II, Post-Synodal Apostolic Exhortation *Pastores Dabo Vobis* (25 March 1992), 29: AAS 84 (1992), 703-705; Benedict XVI, Address to the Roman Curia (22 December 2006): *L'Osservatore Romano*, 23 December 2006, p. 6.

(78) Cf. *Propositio* 11.

(79) Cf. Second Vatican Ecumenical Council, Decree on

Priestly Formation *Optatam Totius*, 6; Code of Canon Law, can. 241, § 1 and can. 1029; Code of Canons of the Eastern Churches, can. 342 § 1 and can. 758; John Paul II, Post-Synodal Apostolic Exhortation *Pastores Dabo Vobis* (25 March 1992), 11, 34, 50: AAS 84 (1992), 673-675, 712-714, 746-748; Congregation for the Clergy, Directory for the Ministry and Life of Priests *Dives Ecclesiae* (31 March 1994), 58; Congregation for Catholic Education, Instruction Concerning the Criteria for the Discernment of Vocations with regard to Persons with Homosexual Tendencies in view of their Admission to the Seminary and to Holy Orders (4 November 2005): AAS 97 (2005), 1007-1013.

(80) Cf. *Propositio* 12; John Paul II, Post-Synodal Apostolic Exhortation *Pastores Dabo Vobis* (25 March 1992), 41: AAS 84 (1992), 726-729.

(81) Second Vatican Ecumenical Council, Dogmatic Constitution on the Church *Lumen Gentium*, 29.

(82) Cf. *Propositio* 38.

(114) Cf. *Propositio* 2.

(115) Cf. *Propositio* 25.

(116) Cf. *Propositio* 19. *Propositio* 25 states: 'An authentic liturgical action expresses the sacredness of the eucharistic mystery. This should be evident from the words and actions of the priest who celebrates, as he intercedes to God the Father both with the faithful and on their behalf.'

(117) *General Instruction of the Roman Missal*, 22; Second Vatican Ecumenical Council, Constitution on the Sacred Liturgy *Sacrosanctum Concilium*, 41; cf. Congregation for Divine Worship and the Discipline of the Sacraments, Instruction *Redemptionis Sacramentum* (25 March 2004), 19-25: AAS 96 (2004), 555-557.

(118) Cf. Second Vatican Ecumenical Council, Decree on the

Pastoral Office of Bishops in the Church *Christus Dominus,* 14; Constitution on the Sacred Liturgy *Sacrosanctum Concilium,* 41.

(119) *General Instruction of the Roman Missal,* 22.

(120) Cf. ibid.

(121) Cf. *Propositio* 25.

(139) *General Instruction of the Roman Missal,* 29; cf. Second Vatican Ecumenical Council, Constitution on the Sacred Liturgy *Sacrosanctum Concilium,* 7, 33, 52.

(140) Cf. *Propositio* 19.

(141) Second Vatican Ecumenical Council, Constitution on the Sacred Liturgy *Sacrosanctum Concilium,* 52.

(142) Second Vatican Ecumenical Council, Dogmatic Constitution on Divine Revelation *Dei Verbum,* 21.

(143) To this end the Synod has called for the preparation of pastoral aids based on the three-year lectionary, to help connect the proclamation of the readings with the doctrine of the faith; cf. *Propositio* 19.

(158) Cf. Congregation for the Clergy, Instruction on Certain Questions Regarding the Collaboration of the Non-Ordained Faithful in the Ministry of Priests *Ecclesiae de Mysterio* (15 August 1997): AAS 89 (1997), 852-877.

(159) Cf. *Propositio* 33.

(160) *General Instruction of the Roman Missal,* 92.

(161) Cf. ibid., 94.

(162) Cf. Second Vatican Ecumenical Council, Decree on the Apostolate of the Laity *Apostolicam Actuositatem,* 24; *General Instruction of the Roman Missal,* 95-111; Congregation for Divine Worship and the Discipline of the Sacraments, Instruction *Redemptionis Sacramentum* (25 March 2004), 43-47: AAS 96 (2004), 564-566; *Propositio* 33: 'These ministries must be introduced in accordance with a specific mandate and

in accordance with the real needs of the celebrating community. Those entrusted with these liturgical services must be chosen with care, well prepared, and provided with ongoing formation. Their appointment must be for a limited term. They must be known to the community and be gratefully acknowledged by the community.'

(222) *The Roman Pontifical, Rites of Ordination of a Bishop, of Priests and of Deacons*, Ordination of a Priest, No. 163.
(223) Cf. John Paul II, Post-Synodal Apostolic Exhortation *Pastores Dabo Vobis* (25 March 1992), 19-33, 70-81: AAS 84 (1992), 686-712, 778-800.
(224) *Propositio* 38.

IV.
VOCATIONS DAY MESSAGES

MESSAGE FOR THE 43rd WORLD DAY OF PRAYER FOR VOCATIONS [36]

7 May 2006 – Fourth Sunday of Easter

Vocation in the mystery of the Church

The celebration of the coming World Day of Prayer for Vocations gives me the opportunity to invite the entire People of God to reflect on the theme *Vocation in the mystery of the Church*. The Apostle Paul writes: 'Blessed be the God and Father of our Lord Jesus Christ . . . even as he chose us in him before the foundation of the world . . . He destined us in love to be his sons through Jesus Christ' (Eph 1: 3-5). Before the creation of the world, before our coming into existence, the heavenly Father chose us personally, calling us to enter into a filial relationship with him, through Jesus, the Incarnate Word, under the guidance of the Holy Spirit. Dying for us, Jesus introduced us into the mystery of the Father's love, a love which completely envelops his Son and which he offers to all of us. In this way, united with Jesus, the Head, we form a sole body, the Church.

The weight of two millennia of history makes it difficult to grasp the novelty of this captivating mystery of divine adoption, which is at the centre of St Paul's teaching. As the Apostle reminds us, the Father 'has made known to us the mystery of his will . . . as a plan to unite all things in him' (Eph 1: 9-10). And he adds, with enthusiasm: 'In everything God works for

---

36. Published 5 March 2006.

good with those who love him, who are called according to his purpose. For those whom he foreknew he also predestined to be conformed to the image of his Son, in order that he might be the first-born among many brethren' (Rom 8: 28-29). The vision is indeed fascinating: we are called to live as brothers and sisters of Jesus, to feel that we are sons and daughters of the same Father. This is a gift that overturns every purely human idea and plan. The confession of the true faith opens wide our minds and hearts to the inexhaustible mystery of God, which permeates human existence. What should be said therefore of the temptation, which is very strong nowadays, to feel that we are self-sufficient to the point that we become closed to God's mysterious plan for each of us? The love of the Father, which is revealed in the person of Christ, puts this question to us.

In order to respond to the call of God and start on our journey, it is not necessary to be already perfect. We know that the prodigal son's awareness of his own sin allowed him to set out on his return journey and thus feel the joy of reconciliation with the Father. Weaknesses and human limitations do not present an obstacle, as long as they help make us more aware of the fact that we are in need of the redeeming grace of Christ. This is the experience of St Paul who confessed: 'I will all the more gladly boast of my weaknesses, that the power of Christ may rest upon me' (II Cor 12: 9). In the mystery of the Church, the mystical Body of Christ, the divine power of love changes the heart of man, making him able to communicate the love of God to his brothers and sisters. Throughout the centuries many men and women, transformed by divine love, have consecrated their lives to the cause of the Kingdom. Already on the shores of the Sea of Galilee, many allowed themselves to be won by Jesus: they were in search of healing in body or spirit, and they were touched by the power of his grace. Others were chosen personally by him and became his apostles. We also find some, like Mary Magdalene and others, who followed him on their own initiative, simply out of love. Like the disciple John, they too found a special place in his heart. These men and women, who knew the mystery of the love of the Father through Jesus, represent the variety of vocations which have always been present in the Church. The model of one called to give witness in a particular manner to the love of God, is Mary, the Mother of Jesus, who in her pilgrimage of faith is directly associated with the mystery of the Incarnation and Redemption.

In Christ, the Head of the Church, which is his Body, all Christians form 'a chosen race, a royal priesthood, a holy nation, God's own people, that you may declare the wonderful deeds of him' (I Pt 2: 9). The Church is holy, even if her members need to be purified, in order that holiness, which is a gift of God, can shine forth from them with its full splendour. The Second Vatican Council highlights the universal call to holiness, when it affirms: 'The followers of Christ are called by God, not because of their works, but according to his own purpose and grace. They are justified in the Lord Jesus, because in the Baptism of faith they truly become sons of God and sharers in the divine nature. In this way, they are really made holy' (*Lumen Gentium*, 40). Within the framework of this universal call, Christ, the High Priest, in his solicitude for the Church calls persons in every generation who are to care for his people. In particular, he calls to the ministerial priesthood men who are to exercise a fatherly role, the source of which is within the very fatherhood of God (cf. Eph 3: 14). The mission of the priest in the Church is irreplaceable. Therefore, even if in some regions there is a scarcity of clergy, it should never be doubted that Christ continues to raise up men who, like the Apostles, leaving behind all other work, dedicate themselves completely to the celebration of the sacred mysteries, to the preaching of the Gospel and to pastoral ministry. In the Apostolic Exhortation *Pastores Dabo Vobis*, my venerable Predecessor Pope John Paul II wrote in this regard: 'The relation of the priest to

Jesus Christ, and in him to his Church, is found in the very being of the priest by virtue of his sacramental consecration/anointing and in his activity, that is, in his mission or ministry. In particular, "the priest minister is the servant of Christ present in the Church as *mystery, communion and mission*. In virtue of his participation in the 'anointing' and 'mission' of Christ, the priest can continue Christ's prayer, word, sacrifice and salvific action in the Church. In this way, the priest is a *servant of the Church as mystery* because he actuates the Church's sacramental signs of the presence of the risen Christ" ' (n.16).

Another special vocation, which occupies a place of honour in the Church, is the call to the consecrated life. Following the example of Mary of Bethany who 'sat at the Lord's feet and listened to his teaching' (Lk 10: 39), many men and women consecrate themselves to a total and exclusive following of Christ. Although they undertake various services in the field of human formation and care of the poor, in teaching or in assisting the sick, they do not consider these activities as the principal purpose of their life, since, as the Code of Canon Law well underlines, 'the first and foremost duty of all religious is to be the contemplation of divine things and assiduous union with God in prayer' (can. 663 §1). Moreover, in the Apostolic Exhortation *Vita Consecrata* Pope John Paul II noted: 'In the Church's tradition religious profession is considered to be a special and fruitful deepening of the consecration received in Baptism, inasmuch as it is the means by which the close union with Christ already begun in Baptism develops in the gift of a fuller, more explicit and authentic configuration to him through the profession of the evangelical counsels' (n. 30).

Remembering the counsel of Jesus: 'The harvest is plentiful, but the labourers are few; pray therefore the Lord of the harvest to send out labourers into his harvest' (Mt 9: 37), we readily recognise the need to pray for vocations to the priesthood and to the consecrated life. It is not surprising that, where people pray fervently, vocations flourish. The holiness of the Church depends essentially on union with Christ and on being open to the mystery of grace that operates in the hearts of believers. Therefore, I invite all the faithful to nurture an intimate relationship with Christ, Teacher and Pastor of his people, by imitating Mary who kept the divine mysteries in her heart and pondered them constantly (cf. Lk 2: 19). Together with her, who occupies a central position in the mystery of the Church, we pray:

O Father, raise up among Christians
abundant and holy vocations to the priesthood,
who keep the faith alive
and guard the blessed memory of your Son Jesus
through the preaching of his word
and the administration of the Sacraments,
with which you continually renew your faithful.
Grant us holy ministers of your altar,
who are careful and fervent guardians of the Eucharist,
the sacrament of the supreme gift of Christ
for the redemption of the world.
Call ministers of your mercy,
who, through the sacrament of Reconciliation,
spread the joy of your forgiveness.
Grant, O Father, that the Church may welcome with joy
the numerous inspirations of the Spirit of your Son
and, docile to his teachings,
may she care for vocations to the ministerial priesthood
and to the consecrated life.
Sustain the bishops, priests and deacons,
consecrated men and women, and all the baptized in Christ,
so that they may faithfully fulfil their mission
at the service of the Gospel.
This we pray through Christ our Lord. Amen.
Mary, Queen of Apostles, pray for us.

MESSAGE FOR THE 44th WORLD DAY OF PRAYER FOR VOCATIONS [37]

29th April 2007 – Fourth Sunday of Easter

'The vocation to the service of the Church as communion'

The annual World Day of Prayer for Vocations is an appropriate occasion for highlighting the importance of vocations in the life and mission of the Church, as well as for intensifying our prayer that they may increase in number and quality. For the coming celebration, I would like to draw the attention of the whole people of God to the following theme, which is more topical than ever: *the vocation to the service of the Church as communion.*

Last year, in the Wednesday general audiences, I began a new series of catechesis dedicated to the relationship between Christ and the Church. I pointed out that the first Christian community was built, in its original core, when some fishermen of Galilee, having met Jesus, let themselves be conquered by his gaze and his voice, and accepted his pressing invitation: 'Follow me and I will make you become fishers of men!' (Mk 1: 17; cf. Mt 4: 19). In fact, God has always chosen some individuals to work with him in a more direct way, in order to accomplish his plan of salvation. In the Old Testament, in the beginning, he called Abraham to form a 'great nation' (Gn 12: 2); afterwards, he called Moses to free Israel from the slavery of Egypt (cf. Ex 3: 10). Subsequently, he designated other persons, especially the

---

37. Published 10 February 2007.

prophets, to defend and keep alive the covenant with his people. In the New Testament, Jesus, the promised Messiah, invited each of the Apostles to be with him (cf. Mk 3: 14) and to share his mission. At the Last Supper, while entrusting them with the duty of perpetuating the memorial of his death and resurrection until his glorious return at the end of time, he offered for them to his Father this heart-broken prayer: 'I made known to them your name, and I will make it known, that the love with which you have loved me may be in them, and I in them' (Jn 17: 26). The mission of the Church, therefore, is founded on an intimate and faithful communion with God.

The Second Vatican Council's Constitution *Lumen Gentium* describes the Church as 'a people made one with the unity of the Father, the Son and the Holy Spirit' (n. 4), in which is reflected the very mystery of God. This means that the love of the Trinity is reflected in her. Moreover, thanks to the work of the Holy Spirit, all the members of the Church form 'one body and one spirit' in Christ. This people, organically structured under the guidance of its Pastors, lives the mystery of communion with God and with the brethren, especially when it gathers for the Eucharist. The Eucharist is the source of that ecclesial unity for which Jesus prayed on the eve of his passion: 'Father . . . that they also may be one in us, so that the world may believe that you have sent me' (Jn 17: 21). This intense communion favours the growth of generous vocations at the service of the Church: the heart of the believer, filled with divine love, is moved to dedicate itself wholly to the cause of the Kingdom. In order to foster vocations, therefore, it is important that pastoral activity be attentive to the mystery of the Church as communion; because whoever lives in an ecclesial community that is harmonious, co-responsible and conscientious, certainly learns more easily to discern the call of the Lord. The care of vocations, therefore, demands a constant 'education' for listening to the voice of God. This is what Eli did, when he helped the young Samuel to understand what God was asking of him and to put it immediately into action (cf. I Sam 3: 9). Now, docile and faithful listening can only take place in a climate of intimate communion with God which is realized principally in prayer. According to the explicit command of the Lord, we must implore the gift of vocations, in the first place by praying untiringly and together to the 'Lord of the harvest'. The invitation is in the plural: 'Therefore pray the Lord of the harvest to send out labourers into his harvest' (Mt 9: 38). This invitation of the Lord corresponds well with the style of the 'Our Father' (Mt 6: 9), the prayer that he taught us and that constitutes a 'synthesis of the whole Gospel' according to the well-known expression of Tertullian (cf. *De Oratione*, 1,6: CCL I, 258). In this perspective, yet another expression of Jesus is instructive: 'If two of you agree on earth about anything they ask, it will be done for them by my Father in heaven' (Mt 18: 19). The Good Shepherd, therefore, invites us to pray to the heavenly Father, to pray unitedly and insistently, that he may send vocations for the service of the Church as communion.

Harvesting the pastoral experience of past centuries, the Second Vatican Council highlighted the importance of educating future priests to an authentic ecclesial communion. In this regard, we read in *Presbyterorum Ordinis*: 'Exercising the office of Christ, the shepherd and head, according to their share of his authority, the priests, in the name of the bishop, gather the family of God together as a brotherhood enlivened by one spirit. Through Christ they lead them in the Holy Spirit to God the Father' (n. 6). The post-synodal Apostolic Exhortation *Pastores Dabo Vobis* echoes this statement of the Council, when it underlines that the priest is 'the servant of the Church as communion because – in union with the bishop and closely related to the presbyterate – he builds up the unity of the Church community in harmony of diverse vocations, charisms and services' (n. 16). It is indispensable that, within the Christian people, every ministry and charism be directed to full communion; and it is the duty of the bishop and priests to promote this communion in harmony with every other Church vocation and service. The consecrated life, too, of its very nature, is at the service of this communion, as highlighted by my venerable predecessor John Paul II in the post-synodal Apostolic Exhortation *Vita Consecrata*: 'The consecrated life can certainly be credited with having effectively helped to keep alive in the Church the obligation of fraternity as a form of witness to the Trinity. By constantly promoting fraternal love, also in the form of common life, the consecrated life has shown that sharing in the Trinitarian communion can change human relationships and create a new type of solidarity' (n. 41).

At the centre of every Christian community is the Eucharist, the source and summit of the life of the Church. Whoever places himself at the service of the Gospel, if he lives the Eucharist, makes progress in love of God and neighbour and thus contributes to building the Church as communion. We can affirm that the 'Eucharistic love' motivates and founds the vocational activity of the whole Church, because, as I wrote in the Encyclical *Deus Caritas Est*, vocations to the priesthood and to other ministries and services flourish within the people of God wherever there are those in whom Christ can be seen through his Word, in the sacraments and especially in the Eucharist. This is so because 'in the Church's Liturgy, in her prayer, in the living community of believers, we experience the love of God, we perceive his presence and we thus learn to recognize that presence in our daily lives. He loved us first and he continues to do so; we too, then, can respond with love' (n. 17).

Lastly, we turn to Mary, who supported the first community where 'all these with one accord devoted themselves to prayer' (Acts 1: 14), so that she may help the Church in today's world to be an icon of the Trinity, an eloquent sign of divine love for all people. May the Virgin, who promptly answered the call of the Father saying, 'Behold, I am the handmaid of the Lord' (Lk 1: 38), intercede so that the Christian people will not lack servants of divine joy: priests who, in communion with their bishops, announce the Gospel faithfully and celebrate the sacraments, take care of the people of God, and are ready to evangelize all humanity. May she ensure, also in our times, an increase in the number of consecrated persons, who go against the current, living the evangelical counsels of poverty, chastity and obedience, and give witness in a prophetic way to Christ and his liberating message of salvation. Dear brothers and sisters whom the Lord calls to particular vocations in the Church: I would like to entrust you in a special way to Mary, so that she, who more than anyone else understood the meaning of the words of Jesus, 'My mother and my brethren are those who hear the word of God and do it' (Lk 8: 21), may teach you to listen to her divine Son. May she help you to say with your lives: 'Lo, I have come to do thy will, O God' (cf. Heb 10: 7). With these wishes, I assure each one of you a special remembrance in prayer and from my heart I bless you all.

MESSAGE FOR THE 45th WORLD DAY OF PRAYER FOR VOCATIONS [38]

13 April 2008 – Fourth Sunday of Easter

'Vocations at the service of the Church on mission'

For the World Day of Prayer for Vocations, to be celebrated on 13 April 2008, I have chosen the theme: *Vocations at the service of the Church on mission*. The Risen Jesus gave to the Apostles this command: 'Go therefore and make disciples of all nations, baptizing them in the name of the Father and of the Son and of the Holy Spirit' (Mt 28: 19), assuring them: 'I am with you always, to the close of the age' (Mt 28: 20). The Church is missionary in herself and in each one of her members. Through the sacraments of Baptism and Confirmation, every Christian is called to bear witness and to announce the Gospel, but this missionary dimension is associated in a special and intimate way with the priestly vocation. In the covenant with Israel, God entrusted to certain men, called by him and sent to the people in his name, a mission as prophets and priests. He did so, for example, with Moses: 'Come, – God told him – I will send you to Pharaoh, that you may bring forth my people . . . out of Egypt . . . when you have brought forth the people out of Egypt, you will serve God upon this mountain' (Ex 3: 10,12). The same happened with the prophets.

The promises made to our fathers were fulfilled entirely in

---

38. Published 3 December 2007.

Jesus Christ. In this regard, the Second Vatican Council says: 'The Son, therefore, came, sent by the Father. It was in him, before the foundation of the world, that the Father chose us and predestined us to become adopted sons . . . To carry out the will of the Father, Christ inaugurated the kingdom of heaven on earth and revealed to us the mystery of that kingdom. By his obedience he brought about redemption' (Dogmatic Constitution *Lumen Gentium*, 3). And Jesus already in his public life, while preaching in Galilee, chose some disciples to be his close collaborators in the messianic ministry. For example, on the occasion of the multiplication of the loaves, he said to the Apostles: 'You give them something to eat' (Mt 14: 16), encouraging them to assume the needs of the crowds to whom he wished to offer nourishment, but also to reveal the food 'which endures to eternal life' (Jn 6: 27). He was moved to compassion for the people, because while visiting cities and villages, he found the crowds weary and helpless, like sheep without a shepherd (cf. Mt 9: 36). From this gaze of love came the invitation to his disciples: 'Pray therefore the Lord of the harvest to send out labourers into his harvest' (Mt 9: 38), and he sent the Twelve initially 'to the lost sheep of the house of Israel' with precise instructions. If we pause to meditate on this passage of Matthew's Gospel, commonly called the 'missionary discourse', we may take note of those aspects which distinguish the missionary activity of a Christian community, eager to remain faithful to the example and teaching of Jesus. To respond to the Lord's call means facing in prudence and simplicity every danger and even persecutions, since 'a disciple is not above his teacher, nor a servant above his master' (Mt 10: 24). Having become one with their Master, the disciples are no longer alone as they announce the Kingdom of heaven; Jesus himself is acting in them: 'He who receives you receives me, and he who receives me receives him who sent me' (Mt 10: 40). Furthermore, as true witnesses, 'clothed with power from on high' (Lk 24: 49), they preach 'repentance and the forgiveness of sins' (Lk 24: 47) to all peoples.

Precisely because they have been sent by the Lord, the Twelve are called 'Apostles', destined to walk the roads of the world announcing the Gospel as witnesses to the death and resurrection of Christ. Saint Paul, writing to the Christians of Corinth, says: 'We – the Apostles – preach Christ crucified' (I Cor 1: 23). The Book of the Acts of the Apostles also assigns a very important role in this task of evangelization to other disciples whose missionary vocation arises from providential, sometimes painful, circumstances such as expulsion from their own lands for being followers of Jesus (cf. 8: 1-4). The Holy Spirit transforms this trial into an occasion of grace, using it so that the name of the Lord can be preached to other peoples, stretching in this way the horizons of the Christian community. These are men and women who, as Luke writes in the Acts of the Apostles, 'have risked their lives for the sake of our Lord Jesus Christ' (15: 26). First among them is undoubtedly Paul of Tarsus, called by the Lord himself, hence a true Apostle. The story of Paul, the greatest missionary of all times, brings out in many ways the link between vocation and mission. Accused by his opponents of not being authorized for the apostolate, he makes repeated appeals precisely to the call which he received directly from the Lord (cf. Rom 1: 1; Gal 1: 11-12 and 15-17).

In the beginning, and thereafter, what 'impels' the Apostles (cf. II Cor 5: 14) is always 'the love of Christ'. Innumerable missionaries, throughout the centuries, as faithful servants of the Church, docile to the action of the Holy Spirit, have followed in the footsteps of the first disciples. The Second Vatican Council notes: 'Although every disciple of Christ, as far in him lies, has the duty of spreading the faith, Christ the Lord always calls whomever he will from among the number of his disciples, to be with him and to be sent by him to preach to the nations [cf. Mk 3: 13-15]' (Decree *Ad Gentes*, 23). In fact, the love of Christ must be communicated to the brothers by example and words, with all one's life. My venerable predecessor John Paul II wrote: 'The special vocation of missionaries *'for life'* retains all its validity: it is the model of the Church's missionary commitment, which always stands in need of radical and total self-giving, of new and bold endeavours' (Encyclical *Redemptoris Missio*, 66).

Among those totally dedicated to the service of the Gospel, are priests, called to preach the word of God, administer the sacraments, especially the Eucharist and Reconciliation, committed to helping the lowly, the sick, the suffering, the poor, and those who experience hardship in areas of the world where there are, at times, many who still have not had a real encounter with Jesus Christ. Missionaries announce for the first time to these people Christ's redemptive love. Statistics show that the number of baptized persons increases every year thanks to the pastoral work of these priests, who are wholly consecrated to the salvation of their brothers and sisters. In this context, a special word of thanks must be expressed 'to the *fidei donum* priests who work faithfully and generously at building up the community by proclaiming the word of God and breaking the Bread of Life, devoting all their energy to serving the mission of the Church. Let us thank God for all the priests who have suffered even to the sacrifice of their lives in order to serve Christ. . . . Theirs is a moving witness that can inspire many young people to follow Christ and to expend their lives for others, and thus to discover true life' (Apostolic Exhortation *Sacramentum Caritatis*, 26).

There have always been in the Church many men and women who, prompted by the action of the Holy Spirit, choose to live the Gospel in a radical way, professing the vows of chastity, poverty and obedience. This multitude of men and women religious, belonging to innumerable Institutes of contemplative and active life, still plays 'the main role in the evangelization of the world' (*Ad Gentes*, 40). With their continual and community prayer, contemplatives intercede without ceasing for all humanity. Religious of the active life, with their many charitable activities, bring to all a living witness of the love and mercy of God. The Servant of God Paul VI concerning these apostles of our times said: 'Thanks to their consecration they are eminently willing and free to leave everything and to go and proclaim the Gospel even to the ends of the earth. They are enterprising and their apostolate is often marked by an originality, by a genius that demands admiration. They are generous: often they are found at the outposts of the mission, and they take the greatest of risks for their health and their very lives. Truly the Church owes them much' (Apostolic Exhortation *Evangelii Nuntiandi*, 69).

Furthermore, so that the Church may continue to fulfil the mission entrusted to her by Christ, and not lack promoters of the Gospel so badly needed by the world, Christian communities must never fail to provide both children and adults with constant education in the faith. It is necessary to keep alive in the faithful a committed sense of missionary responsibility and active solidarity with the peoples of the world. The gift of faith calls all Christians to co-operate in the work of evangelization. This awareness must be nourished by preaching and catechesis, by the liturgy, and by constant formation in prayer. It must grow through the practice of welcoming others, with charity and spiritual companionship, through reflection and discernment, as well as pastoral planning, of which attention to vocations must be an integral part.

Vocations to the ministerial priesthood and to the consecrated life can only flourish in a spiritual soil that is well cultivated. Christian communities that live the missionary dimension of the mystery of the Church in a profound way will never be inward looking. Mission, as a witness of divine love, becomes particularly effective when it is shared in a community, 'so that the world may believe' (cf. Jn 17: 21). The Church prays everyday to the Holy Spirit for the gift of vocations. Gathered around the Virgin Mary, Queen of the Apostles, as in the beginning, the ecclesial community learns from her how to implore the Lord for a flowering of new apostles, alive with the faith and love that are necessary for the mission.

While I entrust this reflection to all the ecclesial communities so that they may make it their own, and draw from it inspiration for prayer, and as I encourage those who are committed to work with faith and generosity in the service of vocations, I wholeheartedly send to educators, catechists and to all, particularly to young people on their vocational journey, a special Apostolic Blessing.

V.

SEMINARIANS

APOSTOLIC JOURNEY TO COLOGNE ON THE OCCASION OF THE 20th WORLD YOUTH DAY

From the

ADDRESS GIVEN TO THE MEETING WITH SEMINARIANS

Cologne – Saint Pantaleon
Friday, 19 August 2005

'We have come to worship Him' – travelling with the Magi

You are seminarians, that is to say, young people devoting an intense period of your lives to seeking a personal relationship with Christ, an encounter with him, in preparation for your important mission in the Church. This is what a seminary is: more than a place, it is a significant time in the life of a follower of Jesus.

I can imagine the echo that resounds in your hearts from the words of the theme of this 20th World Youth Day – *'We have come to worship him'* – and the entire moving narration of the searching and finding of the Wise Men. Each in his own way . . . , [is] like them: they see a star, set out on their journey, they too must face what is unclear and are able to arrive at their destination under God's guidance.

This evangelical passage of the Wise Men who search out and find Jesus has a special meaning precisely for you, dear seminarians, because you are on an authentic journey, engaged in discerning – and this is a true journey – and confirming your call to the priesthood. Let us pause and reflect on this theme.

Why did the Magi set off from afar to go to Bethlehem? The answer has to do with the mystery of the 'star' which they saw 'in the East' and which they recognized as the star of the 'King of the Jews', that is to say, the sign of the birth of the Messiah (cf. Mt 2: 2). So their journey was inspired by a powerful hope, strengthened and guided by the star, which led them towards the King of the Jews, towards the kingship of God himself. This is the meaning behind our journey: to serve the kingship of God in the world.

The Magi set out because of a deep desire which prompted them to leave everything and begin a journey. It was as though they had always been waiting for that star. It was as if the journey had always been a part of their destiny, and was finally about to begin.

Dear friends, this is the mystery of God's call, the mystery of vocation. It is part of the life of every Christian, but it is particularly evident in those whom Christ asks to leave everything in order to follow him more closely.

The seminarian experiences the beauty of that call in a moment of grace which could be defined as 'falling in love'. His soul is filled with amazement, which makes him ask in prayer: 'Lord, why me?' But love knows no 'why'; it is a free gift to which one responds with the gift of self.

The seminary years are devoted to formation and discernment. Formation, as you well know, has different strands which converge in the unity of the person: it includes human, spiritual and cultural dimensions. Its deepest goal is to bring the student to an intimate knowledge of the God who has revealed his face in Jesus Christ.

For this, in-depth study of Sacred Scripture is needed, and also of the faith and life of the Church in which the Scripture dwells as the Word of life. This must all be linked with the questions prompted by our reason and with the broader context of modern life.

Such study can at times seem arduous, but it is an indispensable part of our encounter with Christ and our vocation to proclaim him. All this is aimed at shaping a steady and balanced personality, one capable of receiving validly and fulfilling responsibly the priestly mission.

The role of formators is decisive: the quality of the presbyterate in a particular Church depends greatly on that of the seminary, and consequently on the quality of those responsible for formation.

Dear seminarians, for this very reason we pray today with genuine gratitude for your superiors, professors and educators, who are spiritually present at this meeting. Let us ask the Lord to help them carry out as well as possible the important task entrusted to them.

The seminary years are a time of journeying, of exploration, but above all of discovering Christ. It is only when a young man has had a personal experience of Christ that he can truly understand the Lord's will and consequently his own vocation.

The better you know Jesus the more his mystery attracts you. The more you discover him, the more you are moved to seek him. This is a movement of the Spirit which lasts throughout life, and which makes the seminary a time of immense promise, a true 'springtime'.

When the Magi came to Bethlehem, 'going into the house they saw the child with Mary his mother, and they fell down and worshiped him' (Mt 2: 11). Here at last was the long-awaited moment: their encounter with Jesus.

'Going into the house': this house in some sense represents the Church. In order to find the Saviour, one has to enter the house, which is the Church.

During his time in the seminary, a particularly important process of maturation takes place in the consciousness of the young seminarian: he no longer sees the Church 'from the outside', but rather, as it were, 'from the inside', and he comes to sense that she is his 'home', inasmuch as she is the home of Christ, where 'Mary his mother' dwells.

It is Mary who shows him Jesus her Son; she introduces him and in a sense enables him to see and touch Jesus, and to take him into his arms. Mary teaches the seminarian to contemplate Jesus with the eyes of the heart and to make Jesus his very life.

Each moment of seminary life can be an opportunity for loving experience of the presence of Our Lady, who introduces everyone to an encounter with Christ in the silence of meditation, prayer and fraternity. Mary helps us to meet the Lord above all in the celebration of the Eucharist, when, in the Word and in the consecrated Bread, he becomes our daily spiritual nourishment.

'They fell down and worshiped him . . . and offered him gifts: gold, frankincense and myrrh' (Mt 2: 11-12). Here is the culmination of the whole journey: encounter becomes adoration; it blossoms into an act of faith and love which acknowledges in Jesus, born of Mary, the Son of God made man.

How can we fail to see prefigured in this gesture of the Magi the faith of Simon Peter and of the other Apostles, the faith of Paul and of all the saints, particularly of the many saintly seminarians and priests who have graced the 2,000 years of the Church's history?

The secret of holiness is friendship with Christ and faithful obedience to his will. St Ambrose said: 'Christ is everything for us'; and St Benedict warned against putting anything before the love of Christ.

May Christ be everything for you. Dear seminarians, be the first to offer him what is most precious to you, as Pope John Paul II suggested in his Message for this World Youth Day: the gold of your freedom, the incense of your ardent prayer, the myrrh of your most profound affection (cf. n. 4).

The seminary years are a time of preparing for mission. The Magi 'departed for their own country' and most certainly bore witness to their encounter with the King of the Jews.

You too, after your long, necessary programme of seminary formation, will be sent forth as ministers of Christ; indeed, each of you will return as an *alter Christus*.

On their homeward journey, the Magi surely had to deal with dangers, weariness, disorientation, doubts. The star was no longer there to guide them! The light was now within them. Their task was to guard and nourish it in the constant memory of Christ, of his Holy Face, of his ineffable Love.

Dear seminarians! One day, God willing, by the consecration of the Holy Spirit you too will begin your mission. Remember always the words of Jesus: 'Abide in my love' (Jn 15: 9). If you abide close to Christ, with Christ and in Christ, you will bear much fruit, just as he promised. You have not chosen him – we have just heard this in the witnesses given – he has chosen you (cf. Jn 15: 16).

Here is the secret of your vocation and your mission! It is kept in the Immaculate Heart of Mary, who watches over each one of you with a mother's love. Have recourse to Mary, often and with confidence.

I assure you of my affection and my daily prayers. And I bless all of you from my heart.

From the

ADDRESS GIVEN TO THE STUDENTS OF ROME'S OLDEST SEMINARY THE ALMO COLLEGIO CAPRANICA

Sala Clementina
Friday, 20 January 2006

'I ask you to keep your eyes fixed on Christ'

To respond to the expectations of modern society and cooperate in the vast evangelizing action that involves all Christians, we need well-trained and courageous priests who are free from ambition and fear but convinced of the Gospel Truth, whose chief concern is to proclaim Christ and who are prepared to stoop down to suffering humanity in his Name, enabling everyone, particularly the poor and all who are in difficulty, to experience the comfort of God's love and the warmth of the ecclesial family.

As you well know, in addition to human maturity and persevering adherence to the revealed truth which is faithfully presented by the Church's Magisterium, this entails a serious commitment to personal holiness and the practice of the virtues, especially humility and charity; you must also foster communion with the various members of the People of God, so that in each one of you the awareness of being part of the one Body of Christ and members one of another (cf. Rom 12: 4-6) may grow.

To achieve this, dear friends, I ask you to keep your eyes fixed on Christ, the Author and Perfecter of faith (cf. Heb 12: 2).

Indeed, the greater your communion with him, the better able you will be to follow faithfully in his footsteps, so that, under the guidance of the Holy Spirit, your love for the Lord will develop in 'love, which binds everything together in perfect harmony' (Col 3: 14).

ADDRESS GIVEN DURING A VISIT TO THE COMMUNITY OF THE ROMAN MAJOR SEMINARY ON OCCASION OF THE FEAST OF OUR LADY OF TRUST

Saturday, 25 February 2006

Mary, Mother of Priests

It really is very beautiful and meaningful that you venerate the Virgin Mary, Mother of Priests, with the special title of *Our Lady of Trust*. It evokes a twofold meaning: the trust of the seminarians who, with her help, set out on their journey in response to Christ who has called them, and the trust of the Church of Rome, especially that of her Bishop, which invokes the protection of Mary, the Mother of every vocation, upon this nursery-garden of priests.

It is with Mary's help, dear Seminarians, that today you can prepare for your mission as priests at the service of the Church. A moment ago, when I paused in prayer before the venerable image of Our Lady of Trust in your Chapel, which is the heart of your seminary, I prayed for each one of you. In the meantime, I was thinking once again of the many seminarians who have passed through the Roman Seminary and have subsequently served Christ's Church with love. I am thinking among others of Fr Andrea Santoro, recently killed in Turkey while he was praying.[39] And I also called upon the Mother of the Redeemer to obtain for you the gift of holiness. May the Holy Spirit, who shaped the priestly Heart of Jesus in the Virgin's womb and later at the house in Nazareth, work within you with his grace, preparing you for the future tasks that will be entrusted to you.

Joseph appears to us ever attentive to the voice of the Lord, who guides the events of history, and ready to follow the instructions, ever faithful, generous and detached in service, an effective teacher of prayer and of work in the hidden life at Nazareth. I can assure you, dear Seminarians, that the further you advance with God's grace on the path of the priesthood, the more you will experience what abundant spiritual fruits result from calling on St Joseph and invoking his support in carrying out your daily duty.

---

39. Fr Andrea Santoro was a priest of the Diocese of Rome who had offered to work amongst the Catholic community in Trabzon, Turkey. On 6 February 2006 he was shot dead at the church of Santa Maria, Trabzon, whilst kneeling in prayer, by a sixteen year-old man.

PASTORAL VISIT OF HIS HOLINESS POPE BENEDICT XVI TO POLAND

From the

ADDRESS GIVEN AT THE MEETING WITH MEN AND WOMEN RELIGIOUS, SEMINARIANS AND REPRESENTATIVES OF ECCLESIAL MOVEMENTS

Czestochowa, 26 May 2006

In the school of Mary

Just as the Apostles together with Mary 'went to the upper room' and there 'with one accord devoted themselves to prayer' (Acts 1: 12,14), so we too have come together today at Jasna Góra, which for us at this hour is the 'upper room' where Mary, the Mother of the Lord, is among us. Today it is she who leads our meditation; she teaches us how to pray. Mary shows us how to open our minds and our hearts to the power of the Holy Spirit, who comes to us so as to be brought to the whole world.

My dear friends, we need a moment of silence and recollection to place ourselves in her school, so that she may teach us how to live from faith, how to grow in faith, how to remain in contact with the mystery of God in the ordinary, everyday events of our lives. With feminine tact and with 'the ability to combine penetrating intuition with words of support and encouragement' (John Paul II, *Redemptoris Mater*, 46), Mary sustained the faith of Peter and the Apostles in the Upper Room, and today she sustains my faith and your faith.

'Faith is contact with the mystery of God', to quote Pope John Paul II (*Redemptoris Mater*, 17), because 'to believe means "to abandon oneself" to the truth of the word of the living God, knowing and humbly recognizing "how unsearchable are his judgments and how inscrutable his ways"' (ibid., 14). Faith is the gift, given to us in Baptism, which makes our encounter with God possible. God is hidden in mystery; to claim to understand him would mean to want to confine him within our thinking and knowing and consequently to lose him irremediably. With faith, however, we can open up a way through concepts, even theological concepts, and can 'touch' the living God. And God, once touched, immediately gives us his power. When we abandon ourselves to the living God, when in humility of mind we have recourse to him, a kind of hidden stream of divine life pervades us. How important it is to believe in the power of faith, in its capacity to establish a close bond with the living God! We must give great attention to the development of our faith, so that it truly pervades all our attitudes, thoughts, actions and intentions. Faith has a place, not only in our state of soul and religious experiences, but above all in thought and action, in everyday work, in the struggle against ourselves, in community life and in the apostolate, because it ensures that our life is pervaded by the power of God himself. Faith can always bring us back to God even when our sin leads us astray.

In the Upper Room the Apostles did not know what awaited them. They were afraid and worried about their own future. They continued to marvel at the death and resurrection of Jesus and were in anguish at being left on their own after his ascension into Heaven. Mary, 'she who believed in the fulfilment of the Lord's words' (cf. Lk 1: 45), assiduous in prayer alongside the Apostles, taught perseverance in the faith. By her own attitude she convinced them that the Holy Spirit, in his wisdom, knew well the path on which he was leading them, and that consequently they could place their confidence in God, giving themselves to him unreservedly, with their talents, their limitations and their future.

Many of you here present have experienced this secret call of the Holy Spirit and have responded with complete generosity of heart. The love of Jesus 'poured into your hearts through the Holy Spirit who has been given to you' (cf. Rom 5: 5), has shown you the way of the consecrated life. It was not you who looked for it. It was Jesus who called you, inviting you to a more profound union with him. In the sacrament of Holy Baptism you renounced Satan and his works and received the necessary graces for a Christian life and for holiness. From that moment the grace of faith has blossomed within you and has enabled you to be united with God. At the moment of your religious profession or promises, faith led you to a total adherence to the mystery of the Heart of Jesus, whose treasures you have discovered. You then renounced such good things as disposing freely of your life, having a family, acquiring possessions, so as to be free to give yourselves without reserve to Christ and to his Kingdom. Do you remember your enthusiasm when you began the pilgrimage of the consecrated life, trusting in the grace of God? Try not to lose this first fervour, and let Mary lead you to an ever fuller adherence. Dear men and women religious, dear consecrated persons! Whatever the mission entrusted to you, whatever cloistered or apostolic service you are engaged in, maintain in your hearts the primacy of your consecrated life. Let it renew your faith. The consecrated life, lived in faith, unites you closely to God, calls forth charisms and confers an extraordinary fruitfulness to your service.

Dear candidates to the priesthood! So much can be gained by reflecting on the way Mary learned from Jesus! From her very first 'fiat', through the long, ordinary years of the hidden life, as she brought up Jesus, or when at Cana in Galilee she asked for the first sign, or when finally on Calvary, by the Cross, she looked on Jesus, she 'learned' him moment by moment. Firstly in faith and then in her womb, she received the Body of Jesus and then gave birth to him. Day after day, enraptured, she adored him. She served him with solicitous love, singing the *Magnificat* in her heart. On your journey of preparation, and in your future priestly ministry, let Mary guide you as you 'learn' Jesus. Keep your eyes fixed on him. Let him form you, so that in your ministry you will be able to show him to all who approach you. When you take into your hands the Eucharistic Body of Jesus so as to nourish his People, and when you assume responsibility for that part of the Mystical Body which will be entrusted to you, remember the attitude of wonder and adoration which characterized Mary's faith. As she in her solicitous, maternal love for Jesus, preserved her virginal love filled with wonder, so also you, as you genuflect at the moment of consecration, preserve in your soul the ability to wonder and to adore. Know how to recognize in the People of God entrusted to you the signs of Christ's presence. Be mindful and attentive to the signs of holiness which God will show you among the faithful. Do not fear future duties or the unknown! Do not fear that words will fail you or that you will encounter rejection! The world and the Church need priests, holy priests.

When the Apostles, filled with the Holy Spirit, went out to the whole world proclaiming the Gospel, one of them, John, the Apostle of love, took Mary into his home (cf. Jn 19: 27). It was precisely because of his profound bond with Jesus and

with Mary, that he could so effectively insist on the truth that
'God is love' (I Jn 4: 8,16). These were the words that I placed
at the beginning of the first Encyclical of my Pontificate: *Deus
Caritas Est*! This is the most important, most central truth about
God. To all for whom it is difficult to believe in God, I say again
today: 'God is love'. Dear friends, be witnesses to this truth. You
will surely be so if you place yourselves in the school of Mary.
Beside her you will experience for yourselves that God is love,
and you will transmit this message to the world with the richness
and the variety that the Holy Spirit will know how to enkindle.

Praised be Jesus Christ.

From the

ADDRESS GIVEN DURING THE VISIT TO THE COMMUNITY OF THE ROMAN MAJOR SEMINARY ON OCCASION OF THE FEAST OF OUR LADY OF TRUST

Saturday, 17 February 2007

Gregorpaolo Stano, Diocese of Oria (First-Year Philosopy):
Your Holiness, ours is the first of two years dedicated to discernment, during which we are taught to make a profound personal examination. It is a tiring exercise for us, because the language of God is special, and only those who are attentive are able to discern it among the thousands of voices clamouring inside us. We are asking you, therefore, to help us to understand how God talks in practice and what clues he gives you when speaking to your inmost self?

Pope Benedict XVI: . . . how can we distinguish God's voice from among the thousands of voices we hear each day in our world. I would say: God speaks with us in many different ways. He speaks through others, through friends, parents, pastors, priests. Here, the priests to whom you are entrusted, who are guiding you.

He speaks by means of the events in our life, in which we are able to discern God's touch; he speaks also through nature, creation, and he speaks, naturally and above all, through his Word, in Sacred Scripture, read in the communion of the

Church and read personally in conversation with God.

It is important to read Sacred Scripture in a very personal way, and really, as St Paul says, not as a human word or a document from the past as we read Homer or Virgil, but as God's Word which is ever timely and speaks to me. It is important to learn to understand in a historical text, a text from the past, the living Word of God, that is, to enter into prayer and thus read Sacred Scripture as a conversation with God.

St Augustine often says in his homilies: I knocked on various occasions at the door of this Word until I could perceive what God himself was saying to me. It is of paramount importance to combine this very personal reading, this personal talk with God in which I search for what the Lord is saying to me, and in addition to this personal reading, reading it in the community is very important because the living subject of Sacred Scripture is the People of God, it is the Church.

This Scripture was not simply restricted to great writers – even if the Lord always needs the person and his personal response – but it developed with people who were travelling together on the journey of the People of God and thus, their words are expressions of this journey, of this reciprocity of God's call and the human response.

Thus, the subject lives today as it lived at that time so that Scripture does not belong to the past, because its subject, the People of God inspired by this same God, is always the same, and therefore the Word is always alive in the living subject.

It is consequently important to read Sacred Scripture and experience Sacred Scripture in the communion of the Church, that is, with all the great witnesses of this Word, beginning with the first Fathers and ending with today's Saints, with today's Magisterium.

Above all, it is a Word that becomes vital and alive in the Liturgy. I would say, therefore, that the Liturgy is the privileged place where every one of us can enter into the 'we' of the sons of God, in conversation with God. This is important. The Our Father begins with the words: 'Our Father'; only if I am integrated into the 'we' of this 'Our' can I find the Father; only within this 'we', which is the subject of the prayer of the Our Father, do we hear the Word of God clearly.

Thus, this seems to me most important: the Liturgy is the privileged place where the Word is alive, is present, indeed, where the Word, the *Logos*, the Lord, speaks to us and gives himself into our hands; if we are ready to listen to the Lord in this great communion of the Church of all times, we find him. He opens the door to us little by little.

I would say, therefore, that this is the focus for all the other points: we are personally directed on our journey by the Lord, and at the same time we live in the great 'we' of the Church, where the Word of God is alive.

Moreover, other points are associated with it: listening to friends, listening to the priests who guide us, listening to the voice of today's Church; hence, listening to the voice of the events of this time and of creation which become decipherable in this profound context.

To sum up, therefore, I would say that God speaks to us in many ways. It is important to be in the 'we' of the Church, in the 'we' of the life of the Liturgy. It is important that I personalize this 'we' in myself; it is important to be attentive to the other voices of the Lord, also letting ourselves be guided by the people who have experience of God, so to speak, and help us on this journey, so that this 'we' becomes my 'we', and I become one who truly belongs to this 'we'.

Thus, discernment grows, and personal friendship with God grows, the capacity to distinguish God's voice among the thousands of voices of today, which is always present and always speaks with us.

Claudio Fabbri, Diocese of Rome (Second-Year Philosophy):
Holy Father, how was the period of your formation to the priesthood organized? What interests did you cultivate? Considering the experience you have had, what are the cardinal points of priestly formation? In particular, what place does Mary occupy in it?

Pope Benedict XVI: I think that our life at our seminary in Freising was organized in a very similar way to yours, even if I do not know your exact daily schedule. I think the day began at 6: 30 or 7 a.m. with a half hour's meditation, when each one spoke silently with the Lord, trying to prepare his soul for the Sacred Liturgy. Holy Mass followed, breakfast, and then the morning lessons.

In the afternoon, seminars, study time, and then again common prayer. In the evening, the so-called *'puncta'*, which is when the spiritual director or rector of the seminary spoke to us on various evenings to help us discover the path of meditation; they did not give us a meditation composed in advance, but elements that might help each one of us personalize the Word of the Lord that was to be the object of our meditation.

This was the daily itinerary; then naturally, there were the great feast days with a beautiful liturgy, music. . . . But it seems to me, and perhaps I will return to this at the end, that it is very important to have a discipline that precedes me and not to have to decide again, every day, what to do and how to live. There is a rule, a set discipline that waits for me and helps me live this in an orderly way.

Now, as to my preferences, naturally I followed the lessons with attention, as best I could. Initially, in the first two years of philosophy, it was above all the figure of St Augustine who fascinated me from the very start, then also the Augustinian current in the Middle Ages: St Bonaventure, the great Franciscans, the figure of St Francis of Assisi.

Above all, I found St Augustine's great humanity fascinating, because from the outset as a catechumen he was simply unable to identify with the Church, but instead had to have a spiritual struggle to find, little by little, access to the Word of God, to life with God, until he said his great 'yes' to his Church.

This journey is so human. In it, we can also today see how one begins to enter into contact with God, how all the forms of our natural resistance must be taken seriously and then channelled to arrive at the great 'yes' to the Lord. Thus, his theology conquered me in a very personal way, developed above all by preaching.

This is important because at the outset Augustine wanted to live a purely contemplative life, to write more books on philosophy . . . but the Lord did not want him to, he made Augustine a priest and bishop and so for the rest of his life, his work developed essentially in dialogue with a very simple people.

Moreover, he must have always personally discovered the meaning of the Scriptures, and likewise, must have taken this people's ability, their life context, into account to arrive at a realistic and at the same time very profound Christianity.

Then, naturally, for me exegesis was very important: we had two somewhat liberal but nevertheless great exegetes, also true believers, who fascinated us. I can say that Sacred Scripture really was the soul of our theological studies: we truly lived with Sacred Scripture and learned to love it, to converse with it.

I have already spoken of Patristics, of the encounter with the Fathers. Our dogmatics professor was also a very famous person and had nourished his dogmatics with the Fathers and with the Liturgy.

In his opinion, our liturgical formation was a very central point: there were still no liturgical faculties at that time, but our professor of pastoral studies gave us great courses in liturgy, and at the time he was also rector of the seminary, so the liturgy was lived and celebrated, and thus liturgy taught and thought went together. These, together with Sacred Scripture, were the crucial points of our theological formation. I am always thankful to the Lord for this, because together they truly are the centre of a priestly life.

Another interest was literature: it was obligatory to read Dostoevsky, it was fashionable at that time; then there were also the great French writers: Claudel, Mauriac, Bernanos and also German literature. Furthermore, there was a German edition of Manzoni: at that time I did not speak Italian. So it was that in this sense we gave some sort of form to our human horizon.

Another great love was music, as well as the natural beauty of our land. With these preferences, these realities, I forged ahead on a journey that was not always easy. The Lord helped me to arrive as far as the 'yes' of the priesthood, a 'yes' that has accompanied me every day of my life.

Gianpiero Savino, Diocese of Taranto (First-Year Theology):
In the eyes of most people we might appear as young men who say their 'yes' firmly and courageously and leave everything to follow the Lord; but we know that we are far from being truly consistent with that 'yes'. Trusting as sons, we confess to you the incompleteness of our response to Jesus' call and the daily effort of living a vocation that we feel is propelling us along the path of the definitive and the total [response]. How can we respond to such a demanding vocation as that of shepherds of God's holy People while being constantly aware of our weakness and inconsistencies?

Pope Benedict XVI: It is good to recognize one's weakness because in this way we know that we stand in need of the Lord's grace. The Lord comforts us. In the Apostolic College there was not only Judas but also the good Apostles; yet, Peter fell and many times the Lord reprimanded the Apostles for their slowness, the closure of their hearts and their scant faith. He therefore simply shows us that none of us is equal to this great yes, equal to celebrating *'in persona Christi'*, to living coherently in this context, to being united to Christ in his priestly mission.

To console us, the Lord has also given us these parables of the net with the good fish and the bad fish, of the field where wheat but also tares grow. He makes us realize that he came precisely to help us in our weakness, and that he did not come, as he says, to call the just, those who claim they are righteous through and through and are not in need of grace, those who pray praising themselves; but he came to call those who know they are lacking, to provoke those who know they need the Lord's forgiveness every day, that they need his grace in order to progress.

I think this is very important: to recognize that we need an ongoing conversion, that we are simply not there yet. St Augustine, at the moment of his conversion, thought he had reached the heights of life with God, of the beauty of the sun that is his Word. He then had to understand that the journey after conversion is still a journey of conversion, that it remains a journey where the broad perspectives, joys and lights of the Lord are not absent; but nor are dark valleys absent through which we must wend our way with trust, relying on the goodness of the Lord.

Therefore, also the Sacrament of Reconciliation is important. . . . We must accept our frailty but keep on going, not giving up but moving forward and becoming converted ever anew through the Sacrament of Reconciliation for a new start, and thus grow and mature in the Lord by our communion with him.

It is also important of course not to isolate oneself, not to believe one is capable of going ahead alone. We truly need the company of priest friends and also lay friends who accompany and help us. It is very important for a priest, in the parish itself, to see how people trust in him and to experience in addition to their trust also their generosity in pardoning his weaknesses. True friends challenge us and help us to be faithful on our journey. It seems to me that this attitude of patience and humility can help us to be kind to others, to understand the weaknesses of others and also help them to forgive as we forgive.

I think I am not being indiscrete if I say that today I received a beautiful letter from Cardinal Martini: I had congratulated him on his 80th birthday – we are the same age; in thanking me he wrote: 'I thank the Lord above all for the gift of perseverance. Today,' he writes, 'good is done rather *ad tempus, ad experimentum.*[40] Good, in accordance with its essence, can only be done definitively; but to do it definitively we need the grace of perseverance. I pray each day,' he concluded, 'that the Lord will grant me this grace.'

I return to St Augustine: at first he was content with the grace of conversion; then he discovered the need for another grace, the grace of perseverance, one which we must ask the Lord for each day; but since – I return to what Cardinal Martini said – 'the Lord has given me the grace of perseverance until now, I hope he will also give it to me in the last stage of my journey on this earth.'

It seems to me that we must have trust in this gift of perseverance, but we must also pray to the Lord with tenacity, humility and patience to help and sustain us with the gift of true 'definitiveness', and to accompany us day after day to the very end, even if our way must pass through dark valleys. The gift of perseverance gives us joy, it gives us the certainty that we are loved by the Lord, and this love sustains us, helps us and does not abandon us in our weakness.

Koicio Dimov, Diocese of Nicopolis, Bulgaria
(Second-Year Theology):
Most Blessed Father, commenting on the Way of the Cross in 2005, you spoke of the dirt in the Church; and in the Homily for the ordination of the Roman priests last year, you warned us of the risk 'of careerism, the attempt to get to the top, to obtain a position through the Church.' How do we face these problems as serenely and responsibly as possible?

---

40. Meaning that good is done for a period of time, in order to experience it.

Pope Benedict XVI: It is not an easy question, but it seems to me that I have already said, and it is an important point, that the Lord knows, knew from the beginning, that there is also sin in the Church, and for our humility it is important to recognize this and to see sin not only in others, in structures, in lofty hierarchical duties, but also in ourselves, to be in this way more humble and to learn that what counts before the Lord is not an ecclesial position, but what counts is to be in his love and to make his love shine forth.

Personally I consider St Ignatius' prayer on this point to be very important. It says: '*Suscipe, Domine, universam meam libertatem; accipe memoriam, intellectum atque voluntatem omnem; quidquid habeo vel possideo mihi largitus es; id tibi totum restituo ac tuae prorsus voluntati trado gubernandum; amorem tuum cum gratia tua mihi dones ed dives sum satis, nec aliud quidquam ultra posco.*'[41]

Precisely this last part seems to me to be very important: to understand that the true treasure of our life is living in the Lord's love and never losing this love. Then we are really rich. A man who has discovered a great love feels really rich and knows that this is the true pearl, that this is the treasure of his life and not all the other things he may possess.

We have found, indeed, we have been found by the love of the Lord, and the more we let ourselves be moved by his love in sacramental life, in prayer life, in the life of work, in our free time, the better we will understand that indeed, I have found the true pearl, all the rest is worthless, all the rest is important only to the extent that the Lord's love attributes these things to me. I am rich, I am truly rich and borne

---

41. This prayer is usually rendered: *Take, O Lord, and receive my entire liberty, my memory, my understanding and my whole will. All that I am and all that I possess You have given me: I surrender it all to You to be disposed of according to Your will. Give me only Your love and Your grace; with these I will be rich enough, and will desire nothing more.*

aloft if I am in this love. Here I find the centre of life, its riches. Then let us allow ourselves to be guided, let us allow Providence to decide what to do with us.

Here a little story springs to my mind about St Bakhita, the beautiful African Saint who was a slave in Sudan and then discovered the faith in Italy, who became a Sister. When she was old, the bishop who was paying a visit to her religious house had not met her. He spotted this small, bent African sister and said to Bakhita: 'But what do you do, Sister?'; and Sr Bakhita replied: 'I do the same as you, Your Excellency.' Astonished, the bishop asked her: 'But what?', and Bakhita answered, 'But Your Excellency, we both want to do the same thing: God's will.'

This seems to me to be a most beautiful answer, the bishop and the tiny sister who was almost no longer capable of working, who were both doing the same thing in their different offices; they were seeking to do God's will and so were in the right place.

I also remember something St Augustine said: All of us are always only disciples of Christ, and his throne is loftier, for his throne is the Cross and only this height is the true height, communion with the Lord, also in his Passion. It seems to me, if we begin to understand this by a life of daily prayer, by a life of dedicated service to the Lord, we can free ourselves of these very human temptations.

Francesco Annesi, Diocese of Rome (Third-Year Theology):
Your Holiness, John Paul II's Apostolic Letter Salvifici Doloris *makes it clear that suffering is a source of spiritual wealth for all who accept it in union with the sufferings of Christ. How can the priest today witness to the Christian meaning of suffering in a world that resorts to every legal or illegal means to eliminate any form of pain, and how should he behave towards those who are suffering without running the risk of being rhetorical or sentimental?*

Pope Benedict XVI: Yes, what is he to do? Well, I think we should recognize that it is right to do our utmost to overcome the suffering of humanity and to help those suffering – there are so many of them in the world – to find a good life and to be relieved from the evils that we ourselves often cause: hunger, epidemics, etc.

However, at the same time, recognizing this duty to alleviate the suffering we ourselves have caused, we must also recognize and understand that suffering is an essential part of our human development. I am thinking of the Lord's parable of the grain of wheat that fell to the ground and only in this way, by dying, could it bear fruit; and this falling to the ground and dying is not a momentary event but precisely a life process: to fall like a seed into the earth and thus to die, being transformed, being instruments of God so as to bear fruit.

It was not by chance that the Lord told his disciples: the Son of Man must go to Jerusalem to suffer; therefore, anyone who wants to be a disciple of mine must shoulder his cross so he can follow me. In fact, we are always somewhat similar to Peter, who said to the Lord: 'No, Lord, this cannot happen to you, you must not suffer.' We do not want to carry the Cross, we want to create a kingdom that is more human, more beautiful, on this earth.

This is totally mistaken: the Lord teaches it. However, Peter needed a lot of time, perhaps his entire life, in order to understand it; because in this legend of the *Quo Vadis?*[42] there is

---

42. *Quo Vadis?* literally means 'Where are you going?' Pope Benedict is referring to a very well known story amongst the people of Rome. According to the apocryphal Acts of St Peter, St Peter, fleeing from certain death in Rome, met the Lord walking towards Rome carrying his Cross. St Peter asked him, 'Where are you going?', the Lord replying that he was going to Rome to be crucified again. Peter immediately returned to Rome to join his sufferings to Christ's.

something true: learning that it is precisely in walking with the Lord's Cross that the journey will bear fruit. Thus, I would say that before talking to others, we ourselves must understand the mystery of the Cross.

Of course, Christianity gives us joy, for love gives joy. But love is also always a process of losing oneself, hence, a process of coming out of oneself; in this regard, it is also a painful process. Only in this way is it beautiful and helps us to mature and to attain true joy.

Anyone who seeks to affirm or to promise a life that is only happy and easy is a liar, because this is not the truth about man; the result is that one then has to flee to false paradises. And in this way one does not attain joy but self-destruction.

Christianity proclaims joy to us, indeed; this joy, however, only develops on the path of love, and this path of love has to do with the Cross, with communion with the Crucified Christ. And it is presented through the grain of wheat that fell to the ground. When we begin to understand and accept this – every day, because every day brings some disappointment or other, some burden that may also cause pain – when we accept this lesson of following Christ, just as the Apostles had to learn at this school, so we too will become capable of helping the suffering.

It is true that it is always difficult, if one who is more or less healthy and in good condition is obliged to comfort someone afflicted by a great evil, whether illness or the loss of love. In the face of these evils with which we are all familiar, everything appears almost inevitably rhetorical and pathetic.

Yet, I would say, if these people feel that we are 'compassionate', that we want to share in carrying the Cross with them in communion with Christ, above all by praying with them, helping them with a silence full of sympathy, love, helping them as best we can, then can we become credible.

We must accept this, as perhaps at first our words appear

purely words. However, if we really live in this spirit of truly following Jesus, we also find the way to be close with our sympathy. Etymologically, sympathy means 'com-passion' for the human being, helping him, praying, and thereby creating trust in the Lord's goodness that also exists in the darkest valley. Thus, we can open our hearts to the Gospel of Christ himself, who is the true Consoler; opening our hearts to the Holy Spirit, who is called the other Consoler, the other Paraclete, who is there, who is present. We can open our hearts not because of our words, but because of the important teaching of Christ, his being with us, and thereby help make suffering and pain truly a grace of maturation, of communion with the Crucified and Risen Christ.

Marco Ceccarelli: Diocese of Rome (Deacon):
Your Holiness, in the coming months my companions and I will be ordained priests. We will move from a well-regulated seminary life to the broader context of parish life. What advice can you give us to enable us to adjust as well as possible at the beginning of our priestly ministry?

Pope Benedict XVI: Well, here at the seminary you do have a very good routine. I would say as the first point that it is also important in the life of pastors of the Church, in the daily life of the priest, to preserve as far as possible a certain order. You should never skip Mass – a day without the Eucharist is incomplete – and thus already at the seminary we grow up with this daily liturgy. It seems to me very important that we feel the need to be with the Lord in the Eucharist, not as a professional obligation but truly as an interiorly-felt duty, so that the Eucharist should never be missed.

Another important point is to make time for the Liturgy of the Hours and, therefore, for this inner freedom: with all the burdens that exist, it frees us and helps us to be more open, to be deeply in touch with the Lord.

Of course, we must do all that is required by pastoral life, by the life of a parochial vicar[43] or of a parish priest or by another priestly office. However, I would say, never forget these fixed points, the Eucharist and the Liturgy of the Hours, so that you have a certain order in the daily routine. As I said at the outset, we learned not to have to plan the timetable ever anew; 'Serva ordinem et ordo servabit te'.[44] These are true words.

Next, it is important not to neglect communion with other priests, with one's companions on the way, and not to lose one's personal contact with the Word of God, meditation. How should this be done? I have a fairly simple recipe for it: combine the preparation of the Sunday homily with personal meditation to ensure that these words are not only spoken to others but are really words said by the Lord to me myself, and developed in a personal conversation with the Lord.

For this to be possible, my advice is to begin early on Monday, for if one begins on Saturday it is too late, the preparation is hurried and perhaps inspiration is lacking, for one has other things on one's mind. Therefore, I would say, already on Monday, simply read the Readings for the coming Sunday which perhaps seem very difficult: a little like those rocks at Massah and Meribah, where Moses said: 'But how can water come from these rocks?'

Then stop thinking about these Readings and allow the heart to digest them. Words are processed in the unconscious, and return a little more every day. Obviously, books should also be consulted, as far as possible. And with this interior process, day by day, one sees that a response gradually develops. These words gradually unfold, they become words for me. And since I am a contemporary, they also become words for others. I can

---

43. This is a term for the assistant priest (curate).
44. *Keep order and order will keep you.*

then begin to express what I perhaps see in my own theological language in the language of others; the fundamental thought, however, remains the same for others and for myself.

Thus, it is possible to have a lasting and silent encounter with the Word that does not demand a lot of time, which perhaps we do not have. But save a little time: only in this way does a Sunday homily mature for others, but my own heart is also touched by the Lord's Word. I am also in touch with a situation when perhaps I have little time available.

I would not dare now to offer too much advice, because life in the large city of Rome is a little different to what I experienced 55 years ago in our Bavaria. But I think these things are essential: the Eucharist, the Office of Readings, prayer and a conversation every day, even a brief one, with the Lord on his words which I must proclaim. And never lose either your friendship with priests, listening to the voice of the living Church, or naturally, availability to the people entrusted to me, because from these very people, with their suffering, their faith experiences, their doubts and difficulties, we too can learn, seek and find God, find our Lord Jesus Christ.

VISIT TO THE ROMAN MAJOR SEMINARY ON THE OCCASION OF THE FEAST OF OUR LADY OF TRUST

From the

HOMILY GIVEN DURING THE CELEBRATION OF FIRST VESPERS

Roman Major Seminary, Rome
Friday, 1st February 2008

Let us look to Mary

We are gathered together for first solemn Vespers of this Marian Feast which is so dear to you. We have listened to some verses from St Paul's Letter to the Galatians in which he uses the expression 'fullness of time' (cf. 4: 4). God alone can 'fill the time' and make us experience the full meaning of our existence. God filled time with himself by sending his Only-Begotten Son, and in him he has made us his adoptive sons: sons in the Son. In Jesus and with Jesus, 'the Way, and the Truth, and the Life' (Jn 14: 6), we are now able to find exhaustive answers to the heart's deepest expectations. Once fear has been dispelled, trust in God, whom we even dare to call *'Abba! Father!'* (cf. Gal 4: 6), grows within us.

Dear seminarians, it is precisely because the gift of being adoptive sons of God had illuminated your lives that you were stirred by the desire to make others share in it too. This is why you are here, to develop your filial vocation and prepare yourselves for your future mission as apostles of Christ. It concerns a unified growth, that, while permitting you to savour the joy of life with God the Father, it makes you feel so much more the urgent need to become messengers of the Gospel of his Son Jesus. It is the Holy Spirit who makes you attentive to this profound reality and makes you love it. All this cannot fail to kindle immense trust in you, for the gift you have received is amazing, it fills you with wonder and profound joy. You can therefore understand the role that Mary also has in your lives, invoked in your seminary by the beautiful title: 'Our Lady of Trust'. Like the 'Son, born of woman' (cf. Gal 4: 4), of Mary, Mother of God, so your being sons of God means that you have her as Mother, as a true Mother.

Dear parents, you are probably the most surprised of all at what is happening in your sons. You probably imagined a different career for them than the mission for which they are now preparing. Who knows how often you find yourselves thinking about them: you think back to when they were children, then boys; to the times when they showed the first signs of their vocation or, in some cases on the contrary, to the years in which your son's life seemed remote from the Church. What happened? What meetings influenced their decisions? What inner enlightenment guided their footsteps? How could they then give up even promising prospects of life in order to choose to enter the seminary? Let us look to Mary! The Gospel gives us to understand that she also asked herself many questions about her Son Jesus and pondered on him at length (cf. Lk 2: 19, 51).

It is inevitable that in a certain manner, the vocations of children become the vocations of their parents too. In seeking to understand your children and following them on their way, you too, dear fathers and dear mothers, very often find yourselves involved in a journey in which your faith is strengthened and renewed. You find yourselves sharing in the marvellous adventure of your sons.

Indeed, even though it may seem that the priest's life does not attract most people's interest, it is in fact the most interesting and necessary adventure for the world, the adventure of showing, of making present, the fullness of life to which we all aspire. It is a very demanding adventure; and it could not be otherwise since the priest is called to imitate Jesus, who 'came not to be served but to serve, and to give his life as a ransom for many' (Mt 20: 28).

Dear seminarians, these years of formation constitute an important time in which to prepare yourselves for the exalting mission to which the Lord calls you. Allow me to underline two aspects that mark your current experience. First of all, your seminary years involve a certain detachment from ordinary life, a certain 'wilderness', so that the Lord can speak to your heart (cf. Hos 2: 14). Indeed, his voice is not loud but rather subdued, it is 'a still small voice' (I Kgs 19: 12). Thus, if the Lord's voice is to be heard, an atmosphere of silence is essential. For this reason the seminary offers space and times for daily prayer; it takes great care of the liturgy, meditation on the Word of God and Eucharistic adoration. At the same time, it demands that you devote long hours to study: in praying and studying you can build within yourselves the man of God whom you must be and whom people expect a priest to be.

Then there is a second aspect of your life: during your seminary years, you live together; your formation for the priesthood also involves this community aspect which is of great importance. In following Jesus, the Apostles were formed together. Your communion is not limited to the present time but also concerns the future: the pastoral action that awaits you must see you joining forces, as though in one body, in one *ordo*, that of priests who, together with the bishop, care for the Christian community. May you love this 'family life' which is an anticipation for you of that 'sacramental brotherhood' (*Presbyterorum Ordinis*, n. 8) which must characterize every diocesan priest.

All this reminds you that God calls you to be holy, that holiness is the secret of the true success of your priestly ministry. From this moment holiness must be the goal of your every choice and decision. Entrust this desire and this daily commitment to Mary, Mother of Trust! This most pacifying title corresponds to the invitation, repeated in the Gospel and addressed to the Virgin by the Angel and then so many other times by Jesus to his disciples: 'Do not be afraid' (cf. Lk 1: 30). 'Do not be afraid, for I am with you,' says the Lord. In the icon of Our Lady of Trust, in which the Child points to the Mother, it seems that Jesus is adding, 'Look at your Mother and do not fear.' Dear seminarians, follow the Seminary curriculum with your minds open to truth, transparency and dialogue with those who guide you. This will enable you to respond in a very simple and humble way to the One who calls you, freeing yourselves from the risk of creating a strictly personal project. Dear parents and friends, accompany the seminarians with prayer and with your constant material and spiritual support. I also assure you all of my remembrance in prayer, as I joyfully impart the Apostolic Blessing to you.

VISIT TO THE ROMAN MAJOR SEMINARY ON THE OCCASION OF THE FEAST OF OUR LADY OF TRUST

From the

ADDRESS GIVEN AT THE CONCLUSION OF THE MEETING WITH THE SEMINARIANS

Roman Major Seminary
Friday, 1st February 2008

'This gift of knowing you'

At Vespers today I was particularly moved by the words of the Psalm in which Israel thanks God for the gift of his command that runs swiftly, and it says: he did not do this for all the others, it is only to us that he has given this grace to know his will, his ordinances.

The Israelites did not regard knowing God's Commandments as a burden or a yoke upon their shoulders but rather as a great gift: in the night of the world, they knew who God was and where to go; they knew which was the path of life.

Together with these words, it is even more important for us Christians to know that the Word of God is no longer solely a commandment but also a gift of love, incarnate in Christ. We can really say: thank you Lord for giving us this gift of knowing you; those who know you in Christ therefore know the living Word and know in the obscurity, in the many enigmas of this world, in the many unsolvable problems, the way to go; we know where we come from, what life is and what we are called for.

And I think that this thanksgiving for the knowledge and gift, the knowledge of God Incarnate, must also awaken the idea: but I must communicate this to others, they too are seeking, they too want to live well, they too long for the right path and do not find it. This is especially because it is a grace and also an obligation to know Jesus and to be given the grace to be called by him precisely in order to help others, so that they too may thank God joyfully, that they may have the grace to know who they are, where they come from, where they are going.

Our Lady of Grace, Our Lady of Trust, gave herself totally to the Lord, with great courage. The priesthood . . . is an adventure in today's world in which opposition and many denials of faith abound. It is an adventure and a very beautiful adventure, because this thirst for God really exists in the depths of the heart.

In the past few days, I received the Greek Catholic Bishops of Ukraine on their *ad limina* visit. Especially in the Eastern region, because of the Soviet regime, more than half the people declare themselves to be agnostic, to have no religion. I asked them: what are you doing, how do they behave, what do they want? And all the bishops answered: they have a great thirst for God and desire to know him, they realize it is impossible to live this way.

Thus, despite all the contradictions, forms of resistance and opposition, thirst for God exists and it is our beautiful vocation to help, to give light. This is our adventure. There are, of course, so many unforeseeable things, so many complications, suffering and everything else. Yet, even Our Lady, at the moment of the Annunciation knew that an unknown path lay before her and, familiar with the prophecies of the Servant of God, well-acquainted with Sacred Scripture, she was able to foresee that this path would also be strewn with much suffering. Yet she believed in the angel's words: do not be afraid because in the end God is stronger, do not even fear the Cross or all the suffering, because in the end God guides us and this suffering also helps us to attain the fullness of light.

Thus, may Our Lady of Trust also give you this great confidence, this courage, this joy of being servants of Christ, of the truth, of life.

Thanks to you all and may the Lord bless you all!

APOSTOLIC JOURNEY TO THE UNITED
STATES OF AMERICA AND VISIT TO THE
UNITED NATIONS ORGANIZATION
HEADQUARTERS

From the

ADDRESS OF HIS HOLINESS BENEDICT XVI AT A MEETING WITH YOUNG PEOPLE AND SEMINARIANS

Saint Joseph Seminary, Yonkers, New York
Saturday, 19 April 2008

'Be holy priests'

The People of God look to you to be holy priests, on a daily journey of conversion, inspiring in others the desire to enter more deeply into the ecclesial life of believers. I urge you to deepen your friendship with Jesus the Good Shepherd. Talk heart to heart with him. Reject any temptation to ostentation, careerism, or conceit. Strive for a pattern of life truly marked by charity, chastity and humility, in imitation of Christ, the Eternal High Priest, of whom you are to become living icons (cf. *Pastores Dabo Vobis,* 33). Dear seminarians, I pray for you daily. Remember that what counts before the Lord is to dwell in his love and to make his love shine forth for others.

APOSTOLIC JOURNEY OF HIS HOLINESS
BENEDICT XVI TO SYDNEY (AUSTRALIA)
ON THE OCCASION OF THE 23rd WORLD
YOUTH DAY (12-21 JULY, 2008)

From the

HOMILY OF HIS HOLINESS BENEDICT XVI AT A EUCHARISTIC CELEBRATION WITH BISHOPS, SEMINARIANS AND NOVICES

Saint Mary's Cathedral, Sydney
Saturday, 19 July 2008

'Believe in the light'

I wish now to turn to the seminarians and young religious in our midst, with a special word of affection and encouragement. Dear friends: with great generosity you have set out on a particular path of consecration, grounded in your Baptism and undertaken in response to the Lord's personal call. You have committed yourselves, in different ways, to accepting Christ's invitation to follow him, to leave all behind, and to devote your lives to the pursuit of holiness and the service of his people.

In today's Gospel, the Lord calls us to 'believe in the light' (Jn 12: 36). These words have a special meaning for you, dear young seminarians and religious. They are a summons to trust in the truth of God's word and to hope firmly in his promises. They invite us to see, with the eyes of faith, the infallible working of his grace all around us, even in those dark times when all our efforts seem to be in vain. Let this altar, with its powerful image of Christ the Suffering Servant, be a constant inspiration to you.[45] Certainly there are times when every faithful disciple will feel the heat and the burden of the day (cf. Mt 20: 12), and the struggle of bearing prophetic witness before a world which can appear deaf to the demands of God's word. Do not be afraid! Believe in the light! Take to heart the truth which we have heard in today's second reading: 'Jesus Christ is the same, yesterday, today and for ever' (Heb 13: 8). The light of Easter continues to dispel the darkness!

The Lord also calls us to walk in the light (cf. Jn 12: 35). Each of you has embarked on the greatest and the most glorious of all struggles, to be consecrated in truth, to grow in virtue, to achieve harmony between your thoughts and ideals, and your words and actions. Enter sincerely and deeply into the discipline and spirit of your programmes of formation. Walk in Christ's light daily through fidelity to personal and liturgical prayer, nourished by meditation on the inspired word of God. The Fathers of the Church loved to see the Scriptures as a spiritual Eden, a garden where we can walk freely with God, admiring the beauty and harmony of his saving plan as it bears fruit in our own lives, in the life of the Church and in all of history. Let prayer, then, and meditation on God's word, be the lamp which illumines, purifies and guides your steps along the path which the Lord has marked out for you. Make the

---

45. At the Mass during which this homily was preached the new principal altar of the cathedral was consecrated.

daily celebration of the Eucharist the centre of your life. At each Mass, when the Lord's Body and Blood are lifted up at the end of the Eucharistic Prayer, lift up your own hearts and lives, through Christ, with him and in him, in the unity of the Holy Spirit, as a loving sacrifice to God our Father.

In this way, dear young seminarians and religious, you yourselves will become living altars, where Christ's sacrificial love is made present as an inspiration and a source of spiritual nourishment to everyone you meet. By embracing the Lord's call to follow him in chastity, poverty and obedience, you have begun a journey of radical discipleship which will make you 'signs of contradiction' (cf. Lk 2: 34) to many of your contemporaries. Model your lives daily on the Lord's own loving self-oblation in obedience to the will of the Father. You will then discover the freedom and joy which can draw others to the Love which lies beyond all other loves as their source and their ultimate fulfilment. Never forget that celibacy for the sake of the Kingdom means embracing a life completely devoted to love, a love that enables you to commit yourselves fully to God's service and to be totally present to your brothers and sisters, especially those in need. The greatest treasures that you share with other young people – your idealism, your generosity, your time and energy – these are the very sacrifices which you are placing upon the Lord's altar. May you always cherish this beautiful charism which God has given you for his glory and the building up of the Church!